AF373955

A Thousand Small Resurrections

Find Courage, Healing, and Light—
Not Despite the Breaking, but Because of It.

Copyright © 2026 by Tammi Gunwall

All rights reserved.

No part of this publication may be reproduced, stored in a retrieval system, or transmitted in any form or by any means— electronic, mechanical, photocopying, recording, scanning, or otherwise—without prior written permission of the author, except in the case of brief quotations embodied in critical articles or reviews.

This book is based on true events. To honor privacy and protect those involved, some names and identifying details have been changed.

Scripture quotations are taken from the Holy Bible, New Living Translation, copyright © 1996, 2004, 2007, 2013, 2015 by Tyndale House Foundation. Used by permission of Tyndale House Publishers, Inc., Carol Stream, Illinois 60188. All rights reserved.

First edition

To those who shaped me—
my grandma Jo,
my mom,
my dad, my stepmom
I've learned and taken strength from you.

To those who stand beside me—
my sister,
my girlfriends
you encourage and enlighten me.

To those who rise behind me—
my daughter,
my nieces, my granddaughters
your courage & love will change the world for a better tomorrow.

Each beautiful soul raising the energies of the collective.

And to the men who've exposed
& expanded my heart—
I am grateful for the lessons you've taught me.

Contents

Introduction

For a long time, I wished away the messy parts of my story. The heartbreaks, the betrayals, the abuse, the physical pains, the nights I cried until I couldn't breathe. I wanted to edit them out like unwanted chapters in a book.

But life doesn't give us the luxury of rewriting the past. What it does give us is perspective. Looking back now, I can see how every shattered piece led me to a deeper wholeness. The very moments I despised became the stepping stones to who I am today. The storms I weathered allowed me to see the most vibrant of rainbows. What I once saw only as endings, I now recognize as beginnings—small resurrections quietly unfolding in the middle of my pain.

The truth is, beauty rarely shows up wrapped in perfection. It hides in the cracks of our struggles, in the resilience we never knew we had, in the lessons carved by pain. What once felt like a curse, I now see as a gift. And maybe that's the invitation for us all: not to erase the mess, but to learn how to see the masterpiece within it. To trust that even in the breaking, something new is rising.

For years, I believed keeping quiet was safer than speaking my truth. But what I didn't know then was that silence doesn't protect your heart, it only suffocates your spirit.

This is where many of us begin: carrying stories we don't know how to tell, wounds we don't know how to name. But healing doesn't start in the silence. It begins when we dare to whisper the words, "This happened. And I overcame."

Every truth spoken becomes its own small rising of the soul.

This book is meant to be a mirror. As you read my stories, I hope you see parts of yourself reflecting back *your* truths, *your* hidden pain, or *your* silenced voice, and the tenderness required to give *yourself* grace, show mercy to the parts of *you* needing to be made new, and reclaim *your* voice. Ultimately freeing *your* soul.

Our stories are not just about survival, they're about finding joy, peace and love in the lessons—not just despite what we've endured, but also because of it.

And this book is, at its heart, a testament to the thousand small resurrections that carry us home to ourselves.

I

The Breaking

Some wounds arrive like shattering.
Sharp, sudden, impossible to gather.
You learn how to breathe among fragments,
careful not to cut yourself on what remains.

WHAT YOU HIDE

TO PROTECT

others

MAY BE THE VERY

THING BREAKING

you.

#AThousandSmallResurrections

1

The Weight of Silence

There's no clear memory of when it first began. Only fragments. The house. The time frame. The same nightmare I've had for years replaying again and again: the faceless man chasing me in slow motion around in circles in our driveway. My legs heavy, my voice gone. I always woke up before he caught me. That dream wasn't just fear. It was my body remembering before my mind could name it.

I was around seven years old. We had just moved into our home in Bloomington, MN and started at a new school a block down the road.

The grooming began gradually. That's how it works. It's the slow erosion of safety. Small moments that didn't feel right but were hard to explain as a child. How sitting on my stepdad's lap or his tickling felt "icky," the way he walked about the house naked with an open robe, or how his hugs lingered too long. His "affection" felt different from what I knew with my dad.

I grew up in a time when kids were told not to be rude. "Give your uncle a hug," or "Kiss grandma goodbye." Refusing affection was seen as disrespectful. I learned early that other people's comfort mattered more than my own instincts.

That mindset silenced me before I even knew I had a voice to use.

As I entered puberty at thirteen, boundaries blurred further. His behavior bolder. My stepdad's gazes grew longer, his kisses softer and wetter, and his hugs holding closer to parts of my body that felt too personal and made my skin crawl. When no one else was around, he'd whisper comments about how I looked or smelled, questioned me about my boyfriends or masturbation, and positioned himself in ways that made me feel vulnerable and uncomfortable.

He monitored when I woke up and when others were asleep or out of the house. Sometimes I'd find him deliberately sitting in the living room watching x-rated movies or looking at a magazine, likely to see my reaction. I froze. I panicked. I retreated. I told myself it would stop. But it didn't. There was even a time when he thought I was asleep on the couch so he attempted to touch my breasts. I rolled over, covering myself, and acted like I was still sleeping.

Each blurred boundary was like a small death—the quiet loss of innocence, intuition, and safety.

One morning before school, it crossed a line further, that I couldn't mentally undo.

Our house had five people and only one bathroom, so my sister and I took turns in the mornings. I usually woke first. As I came downstairs that day, I found him sitting in the dark, touching himself with his eyes fixed on me as I passed through the living room. He wasn't startled. He didn't cover up. It had been calculated.

Panic surged through me. I scurried to the bathroom, locked the door, and tried to steady my shaking hands. Feeling anxious and disgusted, I proceeded to start my shower and get in. But this time, I heard the door unlock. My heart began to race.

My stepdad enforced a rule in our house that you were never supposed to lock the bathroom door. Since we only had one bathroom, it was strictly prohibited to lock it if you were in the shower or getting ready. It was rude to hold up the bathroom should anyone need to relieve themselves. The "lock" of course, was easy to jimmy open but it still didn't stop you from receiving either a terrifying pound at the door like the Feds were about to bust in, or get yelled at for disobeying.

As usual, I always watched the base of the shower curtain to see if I could spot feet at the toilet. I held my breath waiting for the flush and those feet to leave. Time seemed to stop.

This time however, the curtain moved. To my shock and horror, my stepdad entered my shower naked. A wave of panic came over me and I turned my back to him and froze. No words were exchanged as he inched closer to me, attempting to lather my body. I trembled as I could feel his erection on my backside. My body screamed, my heart raced, nausea hit me all at once. I couldn't breathe. My voice silenced by fear. I couldn't call for help. It was like my nightmare: being chased in slow motion, unable to escape, and silenced as if the sound was muted. I rinsed as quick as I could, jumped out, and ran to my room. I sobbed quietly as everyone else was still asleep, then collected myself, got ready for school, and never spoke a word to anyone.

I didn't know it then, but trauma has a way of burying you inside yourself.

For days afterward, sleep was impossible. My anxiety and fear consumed me. I couldn't imagine telling my mom. How could she take the betrayal? What if she left him? What if we had to move? Change schools? How could we afford it? What if our lives fell apart? My silence felt like protection. For her, for my sister, even for the family's stability.

Plus, it hadn't happened again... until it did. Repeatedly for months.

I convinced myself that if I carried this secret, I could spare my mom from heartbreak and shield my sister from harm. That distorted belief became my burden to bear. Groomers are master manipulators. They prey on innocence, compassion, and fear, making you believe their shame is yours to carry. And you start to believe it.

So I buried it.

I was just a child when I learned how heavy silence could be.

It doesn't weigh like a stone in your hands—it seeps into your bones. It wraps around your chest until you forget what it feels like to breathe freely. Silence became my shield, my prison, and my secret language. On the outside, I smiled. On the inside, I carried a storm that no one else could see.

I wish I could say I had a moment of bravery and spoke up. I didn't. Children don't break silence; silence breaks them.

The truth surfaced later, in a way that shattered everything.

—-

The night the silence cracked, everything changed.

Mom woke me in the middle of the night, her voice trembling. She had just returned from dinner where my stepdad confessed that he'd been having an affair and that he'd also had "feelings" for me he couldn't control.

Her questions came fast, her tears faster. I could only nod or whisper affirmations. I'd been keeping my emotions, my pain, and my reality so tightly to myself that I wasn't prepared for it to begin unraveling there in the darkness of my bedroom.

What surfaced that night wasn't the whole story, only enough to name that boundaries had been crossed and I felt unsafe. She did not know the full extent of what I endured. I couldn't give her that. I wasn't ready. I wasn't able.

The days and weeks that followed were a blur of confusion, therapy sessions, and emotional chaos. My mom was heartbroken and desperate to help me, but I couldn't find the words. I had spent so long pretending, suppressing, surviving.

How do you explain to people that the nightmare you lived out and replay in your head at night is the last thing you want to discuss or put words to? The thoughts and emotions alone were already too much. Speaking it out loud made it real again, and I wanted nothing more than to forget.

Then one afternoon, I came home to see my mom and stepdad crying and holding each other on the couch. My world collapsed. I didn't understand how she could comfort the man who destroyed everything.

The irony was that I had stayed silent for her, for the family. When she didn't choose me first, I felt utterly betrayed. So I retreated. I avoided home, avoided conversation, avoided my own emotions. My resentment was palpable. None of the uncovering brought me freedom from my pain. Only a second breaking.

Eventually, my mom left him. But by then, the damage had been done. This taught me that loyalty can wound just as deeply as betrayal. My heart learned that love and pain could coexist, that silence was safer than truth, and that even when the truth finally surfaced, it didn't always bring relief. Sometimes, it just exposed the wreckage you've been living with all along.

My silence had cost me my voice, my sense of safety, and the peace of childhood I could never fully reclaim.

PERSONAL INSIGHT

Looking back now, I understand that silence doesn't protect—it isolates. I believed my quiet endurance would safeguard my family, but it only imprisoned me. Children are never meant to carry the shame of adults or bear responsibilities that are not theirs.

Trauma teaches you to take ownership of what never belonged to you.

I confused loyalty with love and silence with strength. Healing begins the moment you allow truth to exist, no matter how painful it feels.

TAKEAWAY

Many of us learn early to suppress our discomfort or instincts for the sake of peace. But your peace cannot grow in the soil of suppression. Speaking your truth, whether to a trusted friend, therapist, or journal— is not betrayal. It's reclamation. It's saying: *This was not my fault. My story matters. I matter.*

SOUL NUGGETS

- *What you hide to protect others may be the very thing breaking you.*
- *Your body and instincts always know when something isn't right.*
- *Healing begins the moment truth is allowed to breathe.*
- *Your truth can rise even when your voice feels small.*

REFLECTIONS / JOURNAL PROMPTS

1. When have you stayed silent to protect someone else?

2. How has silence appeared in your life: as fear, habit, or protection?

3. What might healing look like if you gave your truth a voice?

4. What would you say to the younger version of yourself who carried that silence alone?

5. If your younger self could be heard today, what would she finally say?

If this chapter stirred something tender or difficult, additional support resources are available at the back of this book. You don't have to navigate this alone.

OUR EARLIEST *memories* AREN'T RANDOM, THEY ARE EMOTIONAL *anchors.*

#AThousandSmallResurrections

2

Fragments of a Childhood

The first thing I remember is the sound—my parents' voices exploding through the house, sharp and shaking the air. Then my little sister's cries rising beneath it. I'm four years old, crouched at the top of the open-riser stairs, pulling my knees to my chest, the green shag carpet scratchy under my legs. My fingers wrap tight around the cold iron railing as I peer through the bars. I can see everything, but none of it makes sense. The tension hits my tiny body like a wave, and I try to make myself small. Smaller than the fear rising inside me.

This is my earliest memory.

For years, it felt like a random fragment—one of those odd childhood scenes you aren't sure is real. But healing work has a way of opening the doors you closed long ago. Years later, when I eventually asked my mom about the apartment, she confirmed every detail. And she confirmed something else:

That fight was our last moment in that home. The end of our family as we knew it.

My parents divorced when I was five. By seven, both had remarried, and my life became split between two households—two realities that shaped me in ways I never understood until much later.

Weekdays were with my mom and stepdad. It was the rhythm of day to day life: school, homework, friends, chores, activities. Mom was my lifeline. She was creative, open, and involved. While my stepdad was more reserved, strict, often distant. Life at our house was colorful, easygoing, but at times, emotionally charged or chaotic. Everything was talked about openly. Hardships weren't hidden. If something was wrong or tensions high, we felt it.

Life at dad's house on weekends was the opposite: quiet, predictable, calm. We had routines: Saturday night shows, Sunday church and lunch at my grandparents', the same restaurants, the same bedtime rituals. Everything felt controlled, orderly, safe. Money talks, daily tasks, or disagreements happened behind closed doors or when we weren't there.

For a child trying to make sense of a world that had just split in two, the contrast was huge.

Without even realizing it, I began to build an invisible pedestal for my dad, the one man I believed would never hurt me, never leave, never cause chaos, never disappoint.

He showed up every weekend. He called and checked in when we got older and our schedules grew busy. He and my stepmom seemed like the model of what a solid couple and marriage looked like. I wanted to be like them: put together, calm, unshaken by life's messiness.

I made the distinction early on that being "easy," "good," and "perfect" kept everything peaceful.

I didn't know it then, but this was the birthplace of my lifelong fear:

If I wasn't perfect, I might lose love.
  If I upset someone, they might leave.

My four-year-old self, sitting atop that staircase, learned that love was fragile.
    That families could fall apart in a single moment.
    That a raised voice meant danger.
    That losing someone could happen without warning.

Those beliefs rooted deep.

And they would shape every relationship I had for decades—until the day I began the long, slow resurrection of my truest self.

PERSONAL INSIGHT

Our earliest memories aren't random. They are emotional anchors. Mine became the beginning of a fear of abandonment, my sensitivity to conflict, and the pressure I put on myself to be "good and pulled together enough" to be kept.

I didn't understand the pedestal I began building for my dad. I didn't understand why his approval mattered so deeply. But a child doesn't need logic. They need stability.

This memory was the first place something in me broke... but it would also be a memory I would one day rise from. Because healing is often a returning to the younger version of yourself who couldn't process what happened, and finally giving her the love and security she longed for.

TAKEAWAYS

Abandonment wounds aren't always caused by dramatic moments. Sometimes they're born from subtle emotional inconsistencies, unspoken expectations, or the quiet ache of wanting to be accepted.

Look back at your earliest memory not with blame, but with curiosity. It may not define your life. It usually defines a pattern.

When you understand the moment your fear began, you can begin the slow, steady resurrection of your truth... the part of you that no longer needs to perform to be loved.

Healing begins the moment you realize:
   You can rise from the places where you once broke.

SOUL NUGGETS

- *Your first wound often becomes your loudest fear, but not your final story.*

- *Children don't just remember events. They remember what their bodies survived.*
- *We learn to perform when we fear being left, but we rise when we learn to stay with ourselves.*
- *Safety shapes us more than love alone.*

REFLECTION / JOURNAL PROMPTS

1. What is the earliest memory you can recall from childhood?

2. What emotions did that younger version of you feel?

3. What belief about yourself or about love may have been born in that moment?

4. How does that belief still show up in your life today?

THE
UNHEALED HEART
DOESN'T SEEK
love,
IT SEEKS WHAT'S
familiar.

#AThousandSmallResurrections

3

When Love Looked Like Safety

I spent most of high school trying to stay busy—friends, boyfriends, dance, work, anything to keep me preoccupied. The less time I spent at home, the safer I felt.

Devin had been in my life since I moved to Richfield in third grade. A few weeks after school started, there was an interruption in Ms. Weston's math class. A new student was joining us. When he walked in, the room buzzed with whispers, *He's back!* Since I was new, I didn't understand why. I soon learned he'd been one of the heartthrobs at Lincoln Hills Elementary.

His best friend, Sam, lived just on the other side of the fence from me. My sister, my girlfriend, and I would sit on that fence, watching the boys play ball while blasting *I Love Rock 'n' Roll* on the boom box. Summers were spent riding bikes until dark, playing Kick the Can, or climbing the dirt pits that later became Centennial Lakes. We thought of ourselves as a little street gang, free until our parents whistled us home.

By fifth grade, a playground trend emerged: full-fledged wedding ceremonies at recess. There were coordinators, bridal parties, dandelion bouquets, even proposals, all squeezed into twenty minutes before the bell rang. Every day, a new ceremony took place. One day, Dev shyly asked if I'd marry him. I really liked him, but I told him I had to ask my mom first.

That night she smiled and said, "I don't think you're old enough for marriage yet."

So the next day, I broke the news. We never had our ceremony, but in some innocent way, that moment marked the beginning of a bond that would weave in and out of my life for years. On the last day of school, he jumped out from behind a bush, planted a big kiss on my lips, and ran away screaming.

It was my first official kiss.

By middle school, life scattered us. Sports and activities pulled us in different directions. Sam moved away, and Dev across town. We saw less of each other, but the thread never fully disappeared.

— -

At the end of eighth grade, I started seeing Nate. He was my first real boyfriend, my first love. His parents were strict and didn't allow us to date, so our relationship existed mostly in secret. At the time, I didn't understand their concern. What I felt instead was the sting of not being chosen openly. Of being hidden.

We snuck moments together whenever we could, and while there was excitement in that, it came at a cost. I spent many hours waiting for scraps of his attention and missing the carefree ease of being a teenager. Looking back, Nate was my first lesson in love that required me to disappear.

Sports also consumed him. His training, weight cutting, and discipline left little room for anything else. Over time, I began noticing habits that scared me—excessive exercise, laxatives, bingeing and purging. I became concerned enough that I eventually told the school nurse. I felt awful, but knew I couldn't stay silent. Though Nate was angry at first, he later thanked me for helping him get the support he needed.

I didn't realize it then, but that was the first time I chose truth over comfort. The first time I spoke up even when it hurt.

We stayed together for nearly two and a half years before our relationship slowly faded. During that time, Dev would call occasionally. He'd flirt, confess his crush for me, and then urge me to leave Nate. He had a reputation. Most girls had either dated him or fooled around with him. I enjoyed the attention but didn't fully trust it. Somewhere deep inside, I already knew the difference between attention and commitment, I just didn't yet trust myself enough to listen.

One night, after a long call, he hesitated for what felt like forever before blurting out that he loved me. I laughed and said, "You don't even know what love is." He was crushed. And never let me forget it.

Nate and I had been broken up only days when Dev caught wind of the news and called again. Junior prom was coming up. He asked me to the dance. I said yes.

We both fell hard. The chemistry was undeniable. We became insepa-rable. After years of sneaking around with Nate, being openly chosen felt intoxicating. Dev wanted to be with me all the time. We laughed, shared inside jokes, gave each other nicknames. To everyone else he was Dev, but to me, he became Devin.

Devin felt like home. A place where I felt seen, wanted, safe. Maybe that's why I ignored the rumors of his cheating. I told myself he had changed. That he was different with me.

After graduation, Devin joined the Marines, and went off to boot camp in San Diego. We wrote letters back and forth. He talked about marriage, about a future together. He proposed not long after his return. I wasn't sure we were ready—but I loved him, and I loved the idea of us.

When I told my mom, she repeated what she'd said years earlier, "Tam, you're too young. This isn't a good idea."

This time, I didn't listen. I was nineteen and certain I could take on the world.

One night, after I went to bed early, I overheard my mom and best friend talking downstairs. Not realizing I could hear them, they spoke about Devin, our relationship, their doubts, and the rumors I'd chosen not to hear. Instead of hearing concern, I felt completely betrayed. Secrets had always shaped my life, and once again, truth was being whispered behind closed doors.

The next day, I packed my things and moved out.

—-

Now stationed at Camp LeJeune, Devin and I decided to elope. So on Memorial Day weekend, we got married at the courthouse in Jacksonville, North Carolina. No family. No ceremony. Just us, and two of his Marine buddies as witnesses.

We agreed I would finish school in Minnesota before joining him, visiting each other when we could. But it wasn't long before things escalated in the Middle East. Devin was to be deployed to Saudi Arabia for the Gulf War. There was no time for another visit. We had to say our goodbyes over the phone. He begged me to take a pregnancy test—he just had a feeling. I thought he was being ridiculous, but the day after he left, I took one anyway.

He was right.

It was the kind of plot twist only life can write: unexpected, terrifying, and beautiful all at once. Just three months after getting married, we were pregnant, but miles apart.

Eight months later, Devin landed safely back in the States. I was swollen like a blimp, and preparing for our daughter's arrival. I wasn't about to keep our family apart any longer, so I quit my two jobs, left school, sold my car, and moved to North Carolina. We rented a small mobile home while waiting for base housing. It wasn't much, but it was ours. Some of my best memories come from that time—when we had next to nothing; sitting on the floor, listening to music, going for walks together, believing like life couldn't get much better.

One Friday night, Devin had a buddy over and they stayed up late drinking while I, exhausted and only days from giving birth, went to bed. Their conversation drifted through the cracked door. They started talking about women. Conquests.

Then I heard my husband.

Casually bragging. Naming women he had cheated with—even since we'd been married. One in particular that he'd worked with.

My heart shattered instantly. It was the kind of pain that takes your breathe away. Laying in the darkness, my tears were uncontrollable. I was nine months pregnant with his child. I had uprooted my entire life for him. For us. And in that moment, I realized I had been silencing my intuition all along.

This wasn't my past unraveling. This was my future collapsing.

My body went cold. Hope drained from me. And my survival instincts—those old, loyal companions—took over.

The next day, I did what I knew best: I went silent. I closed up. Shut down.

Silence had always been my survival language. The place I went when speaking felt more dangerous than staying quiet. I was too ashamed to tell my mom she had been right. Too embarrassed to tell anyone. Instead of turning my anger outward, I turned it back on myself. *This was my fault. I have to stick it out.*

I was pregnant, broke, and alone in a state where I knew no one. Looking back, I see how the girl who tried to outrun pain eventually ran straight into it. Not because I was weak, but because I hadn't yet healed.

PERSONAL INSIGHT

When we've grown up in chaos, love can feel like safety, even when it's not. What we often mistake for love is sometimes just familiarity wrapped in attention. I was chasing the comfort of being seen, not realizing that what I truly longed for was peace. I didn't realize I was choosing what felt familiar, not what felt healthy.

TAKEAWAY

Don't ignore the quiet voice of intuition just because the noise of desire is louder. The parts of you that whisper warnings aren't trying to ruin your happiness. They're trying to preserve your peace. Intuition is the soul's way of remembering what the mind has forgotten.

SOUL NUGGETS

- *Attention isn't the same as affection.*
- *Ignoring intuition is like muting your soul's alarm clock.*
- *Silence may protect you for a time, but it also conceals the truth that sets you free.*
- *If you have to abandon yourself to keep someone, it isn't love.*

REFLECTION / JOURNAL PROMPTS

1. Think of a time when you confused attention or chemistry for love. What did it teach you about what you truly need?

2. What does safety feel like in your body? How is it different from the feeling of being wanted?

3. Where in your life might you still be silencing your intuition to keep the peace?

4. How can you begin listening to the voice within you, the one that's been right all along?

5. Where have you mistaken intensity for intimacy or consistency for safety?

* *For readers seeking support—for themselves or someone they love—a list of trusted resources can be found at the back of this book.*

THE BODY *remembers* WHAT THE MIND TRIES TO *bury.*

#AThousandSmallResurrections

4

The Body Keeps Score

I had done my best to run from all the things that haunted me growing up. I truly believed that if I buried them deep enough, they'd eventually fade away.

But then, I became a mom.

My daughter was born a month before my twenty-first birthday and just days after learning that my husband had been unfaithful. I had run from my past, thousands of miles from home, into a marriage I hoped would save me—only to be betrayed all over again.

She was the only thing that kept me grounded. She was beautiful, perfect, and mine. I could hold her for hours, breathing her in, memorizing her face. I poured every ounce of love and energy I had into that little girl. My world revolved around her.

But that's also when the nightmares came back.

The same recurring dream from childhood: a faceless man chasing me in the driveway of my old home.

Around the same time, my stomach issues surfaced. And when intimacy with my husband sometimes triggered flashes of my stepdad—images I spent years trying to forget. I felt my body pull away before my mind could catch up. I had to keep the lights on just to stay present, reminding myself where I was, anchoring my mind back to my body. Some nights I recoiled from my husband's touch if I couldn't see him.

Oh, how the dark can play evil tricks on a haunted soul.

As I held my daughter, I began to imagine what I would do if anything like what happened to me ever happened to her. That's when the fury found me. It wasn't just anger—it was the voice of the mother inside me, roaring for the girl who had never been protected. Not only for what my stepdad had done, but for what my mom hadn't.

Even as life kept moving, my body refused to let the past rest. Every nightmare, every ache, every panic episode was its way of whispering:

There's still something here to be healed.

— -

Before moving to North Carolina, my mom and I managed to patch things up enough to start talking again. When I moved, she sent letters, care packages, and small comforts from home. I clung to her support as I navigated new motherhood.

We didn't talk much about my stepdad. She knew it was a line I wasn't ready, or willing, to cross. She apologized many times for how her concerns about Devin had hurt me, insisting she had only wanted the best for me. What she didn't know was how deeply I was struggling beneath the surface.

Truthfully, the distance was probably good for both of us. Our relationship slipped back into the way it had always been: talking about everything except the things that mattered most.

— -

Truth, Spoken in Love, Interrupts the Cycle

My sister came out for a visit while I was pregnant with my son.

We were still living in North Carolina yet, far from home, far from the house where silence had been learned and survival had been practiced.

That distance mattered.

Away from familiar walls and old patterns, something softened. I was already tender, my body stretched by pregnancy, my inner world continuing to quietly unravel. And in that space, my sister finally felt safe enough to speak.

After nearly five years of silence, she began to ask questions.

Years earlier, while she was still in high school, she had learned about what happened to me. The truth surfaced quietly, through a conversation she had with our mom. Our mom asked her if anything inappropriate had ever happened to her.
It had.

But she said no.

Later, she told me she had been instantly overtaken by emotion—bawling as the weight of it all hit her at once. Devastation for me. Validation that what she herself had endured was wrong. And the sobering confirmation of what he was capable of. It was too much to process, too much to hold, and she stayed silent.

And I, never knowing she had been told anything at all, stayed silent too.

For five years, we carried our pain separately. We were close, but unable to reach one another past the shadows we didn't know how to name. Each of us believing we were protecting the other by not speaking.

That visit changed everything.

As we talked, I shared the details of my story openly for the first time without minimizing. She listened with a steadiness that told me I was safe. And then, through tears and long pauses, she told me that he had crossed boundaries with her too.

Our stories were different, but both were abuse.

For years, I had prayed that my tolerance—my silence—might somehow protect her. That if I endured it quietly enough, she would be spared.

She wasn't.

The realization crushed me.

I had feared so deeply for her safety, and yet my silence had unknowingly left her alone in hers. The guilt was heavy—not because the responsibility was ever mine, but because love always wishes it could have done more.

And yet, something sacred unfolded in that breaking.

We spoke freely. We validated one another. We shared our truth. Our inner children, once isolated by shame and confusion, were finally allowed to exist in the open, without blame or judgment.

We grieved together. We were angry together. We bore witness to one another's survival.

That conversation became my first true breaking open. Not because the pain disappeared, but because it was no longer carried alone.

It was the moment my story stopped living only inside my body and finally entered relationship.

Being witnessed by someone who shared my history and loved me gave my pain a place to land. What had once been trapped in silence could now move toward meaning.

—-

After my son was born, I had hoped that my symptoms would subside. But they didn't. The nightmares, the stomach issues, the anxiety, the depression continued. My daughter and son were just sixteen months apart. I was a stay-at-home mom while Devin worked long hours on base as a cook. I loved my children, but I felt isolated and lonely. Every time I connected with a neighbor, they were relocated or discharged back to civilian life. Just as I found my footing, the ground would shift again.

Devin was nearing the end of his four-year enlistment with the Marines, and we were preparing to return to Minnesota. He wanted to re-enlist, but I couldn't do another four years so far from home. I needed roots. Family. Familiarity. Connection.

I knew my past was catching up with me. I saw the toll it was taking on my body, my mind, and my marriage. Devin knew about my abuse in the broadest sense—enough to be gentle, patient, and tender when I struggled. I appreciated his understanding.

But the war inside me hadn't yet been won.

PERSONAL INSIGHT

Becoming a mother didn't just change my life, it exposed the places inside me I had long abandoned. I had spent years outrunning memories I didn't want to name, but my body never stopped holding them. The nightmares, the stomach pain, the panic, the flashes during intimacy weren't random outbursts. They were invitations.

My body wasn't betraying me; it was trying to lead me back to the parts of myself still waiting to be acknowledged, honored, and healed. Healing began when my body no longer carried the story alone. When my truth was finally witnessed and spoken in love.

Speaking it openly with my sister did not erase the pain, nor did it immediately quiet my body's symptoms. But it did release me from the isolation that had kept the trauma locked inside me. Something shifted. What had been born in silence could finally be held in relationship. And that was the beginning of my awakening.

TAKEAWAY

Healing begins the moment we stop running from what hurts and start paying attention to the wisdom the body offers. It remembers so that we don't have to live divided.

When pain is shared with someone safe, the body no longer has to scream for attention. It can begin to soften, trust, and rest.

SOUL NUGGETS

- *Motherhood often awakens the wounds we thought were healed.*
- *Your body's symptoms are not punishments, they're messages.*
- *What the mind avoids, the body repeats until it is heard.*
- *You don't heal by forgetting. You heal by finally listening.*
- *Shared truth turns silent suffering into the beginning of freedom.*

REFLECTION / JOURNAL PROMPTS

1. Recall a moment when your body tried to communicate something your mind didn't want to face. What was it trying to protect you from or lead you toward?

2. When you slow down, what emotions, memories, or sensations begin to rise?

3. How has your body carried you through pain you couldn't yet process? What gratitude does it deserve?

4. Where in your life are you still minimizing or dismissing your body's signals? What would it look like to listen more gently?

5. Who has been—or could become—a safe witness to your story? What might shift if you no longer carried it alone?

39

WHEN THE
PAST REFUSES
silence,
THE SOUL
INSISTS ON
truth.

#AThousandSmallResurrections

5

A Past Demanding to Be Faced

We had been home for less than six months before my mom decided to move to Florida. She'd reconnected with an old friend who encouraged her to start fresh, to leave Minnesota and everything tied to it.

Divorced and ready for change, she packed up and said goodbye.

At first, I was angry—frustrated that she was running. From her family. From her past. From the chance to be an active grandma to my kids. But with time, I realized something I didn't want to admit: distance was what kept our relationship intact.

From far away, neither of us had to face the truth we'd buried for years.

In it's own way, her leaving felt like a small death—the closing of a door we had never fully dared to open.

—-

At twenty-seven, I fell into a deep depression. It was the kind of heaviness that presses against your ribs and steals your breath. I looked around at my life—my family, the house, the routine—and thought, *Is this really it?*

Everything looked "right," yet inside, I felt hollow. I couldn't seem to shake the void inside me.

Something in me was trying to rise, but I didn't know how to let it.

So, I turned inward. I began journaling. Reading books on authenticity and purpose. Searching for the root of the ache I couldn't name. The more I wrote, the more I sensed an old version of myself stirring— something I had buried long ago.

As my symptoms intensified, so did the clarity:
it was time to face what I had spent years avoiding.

Motherhood had awakened old pain. And I had questions. So many questions for my mom. Journaling made it undeniable: the truth I'd buried was pushing to the surface. The past wasn't staying quiet anymore.

I booked a flight to Florida, hoping for clarity. Maybe closure. Maybe the apology I had longed for. Maybe a resurrection of something between us that had long been dead.

—-

For two days, we sat and talked. We cried, argued, hugged.
Everything spilled out.
Everything hurt.

It was freeing to finally speak my truth—yet frustrating to realize that even honesty can't force understanding. It doesn't always bring resolution. We were both hurting and trying so hard to explain our perspectives that neither of us truly heard the other.

I got an apology. But it didn't soothe the ache inside me.
 Grief rose where relief was supposed to be.

I left for home, knowing I had moved the needle forward, but healing wasn't a single conversation. It was far from where I wanted to be. It would take a long unlearning: of silence, of shame, of carrying the weight alone.

The truth had risen. But my spirit was still calling out. I had faced the pain of my past but hadn't yet learned how to nurture myself through it. The rebuild would come later through career shifts, new friendships, heartbreak, and the slow, steady rise of my own voice.

PERSONAL INSIGHT

Confronting my mom wasn't really about her, it was about me finally choosing to face the parts of my story I had been avoiding. Speaking my truth didn't bring instant healing or closure, but it awakened something inside me. I learned that healing doesn't come from someone else finally understanding you; it begins the moment you stop abandoning yourself. That conversation was less about closure and more about reclaiming a part of me.

TAKEAWAY

You don't need someone else's apology to begin healing. What you truly need is the courage to honor your truth and release the expectation that someone else will repair what they broke. Freedom begins not with someone else's change, but with your own awakening.

SOUL NUGGETS

- *Truth-telling is a resurrection of the parts of you you once buried.*
- *Healing isn't found in someone else's apology, it's found in your own voice.*
- *Closure is an inside job.*
- *You can't force understanding, but you can choose freedom.*

REFLECTION / JOURNAL PROMPTS

1. Is there a conversation you've avoided out of fear, loyalty, or pain?

2. What part of your truth is rising now, asking to be acknowledged?

3. What would closure look like if you offered it to yourself instead of waiting for it from someone else?

45

THE HEART

DOESN'T

BREAK TO

punish you,

IT BREAKS TO

free you.

#AThousandSmallResurrections

6

When The Heart Cracks Open

A few years after we moved back to Minnesota from military life, I decided to go back to school and complete my Visual Communications degree. It wasn't easy juggling work, family, college courses, and homework, but we needed higher-paying jobs, and my dream was still to work in design.

It had been hard for me to walk away from school early in our marriage. I needed something of my own again to light a spark back in me—some small ember of myself I feared had gone out.

After finishing school, I had a couple of interesting design jobs, but it wasn't until I landed my role working for a nationally syndicated television show, that I really came alive. I'd been a huge fan of the home improvement program—watching regularly when the kids were little. We couldn't afford cable, so we watched a lot of public television. The hosts made DIY projects seem easy, and I often daydreamed about what owning our own house might be like someday.

When I joined their marketing team creating print collateral, managing two ecommerce websites, and designing everything from DIY books to TV graphics, it felt surreal.

My first day there, I got the full tour and met my new coworkers. Many of whom I'd work with for the next seven years, and some who remain friends today. It's also the day I met Anthony.

As Marketing Manager, he and I would be working closely together. He had a light sense of humor and a grounded way about him. From the start, he made me feel at ease. Over time, we grew into close friends. Most days, you could find us eating lunch with a few others or chatting about almost anything from our office doorways or on instant messenger. We were even told once or twice to "chat less and work more."

He challenged and encouraged my creativity, and I valued that deeply. My husband never really asked much about my work or showed interest in that part of my life. So having someone who "got it" meant a lot. Anthony saw my talent and my drive, and I saw his.

Occasionally, we'd hang out outside of work with coworkers and even our spouses. We used to joke about being each other's "work spouse." But truthfully, there was never flirtation. Just comfort, friendship, and mutual respect.

Then one day, during our morning chat, Anthony told me he had accepted a new position—more opportunity, more pay. While I congratulated him, my heart sank. For four years, we'd worked side by side. He was my daily constant, my sounding board, my friend. The thought of him being gone left me hollow. I knew that continuing our friendship the way it had been, outside of work, might raise eyebrows or invite suspicion.

I began to unravel quietly. I couldn't eat or sleep. While others planned his farewell, I was silently falling apart. Within weeks, I'd lost 20 pounds. I told myself I was fine, but my body felt like it was running on adrenaline I couldn't turn off.

That's when I realized what I'd been denying: I loved him.

In a moment of desperation for my sanity and my physical health, I wrote a long message expressing how much I cared for him. How much his absence hurt. And hit send. I thought getting it off my chest might calm my nervous system. I needed to tell someone and figured the safest person to tell was him. I fully expected Anthony to gently remind me that we were both married, that boundaries mattered. Instead, his reply read:

"I've been wrestling with the same feelings."

What I thought would ease my anxiety only deepened my confusion. The truth was, this wasn't just about him. Anthony was simply the spark in a room already filled with fumes. It was the build up of years of endurance, unspoken grief, and unmet needs—the perfect storm I had been bracing against without realizing how exhausted I'd become.

—-

Devin and I had already been through so much in our fifteen years of marriage. Addiction, betrayal, financial strain, anxiety, and depression had all left marks. Like the way glass cracks from a pressure point no one notices until the fracture finally reaches the edge.

I often felt we had been two kids pretending to be adults, learning hard lessons as we went. What most people experience in dating and growth years, we experienced inside marriage. Leaving scars we didn't know how to heal.

Devin's alcoholism seeped into every part of our lives. When he drank, the cycle began. He would disappear for hours—sometimes days—into binges that drained our bank account and destabilized our world. At times there were volatile outburts, fights, impulsive spending, or betrayals that cut deep. But more than anything, it was the disappearing that undid me. Never knowing when, or if, he would return safely. The aftermath always followed: for him panic attacks, days in bed, and me holding together the house, the kids, and whatever pieces were left. When he was sober, things were good. But the unpredictability of when the next storm would hit kept my nervous system always braced.

On one occasion, after an argument over where he'd been all night, I told him that the day I stop caring is the day he needs to worry. And slowly, gradually, eventually, I no longer could hold him up while keeping our family afloat. I loved him, but I couldn't keep repeating this cycle.

Our disconnect had been growing for a long time. I often asked for date nights, hoping to reconnect, but Devin brushed it off. "Married couples don't date," he'd say. And if we did go out, he'd usually end the night by going out drinking with his buddies.

I began to believe the only thing holding us together was our kids and our history. I'd asked repeatedly for counseling, but that too was met with excuses or dismissiveness.

Eventually, I stopped asking. I stopped trying.

Not long after realizing my deeper feelings for Anthony, I decided to have an honest conversation with Devin. I told him I was scared for the state of our marriage. I had begged for us to fight for it for so long, but now feared I was past the point of no return.

In that moment, it became clear: what I had been yearning for was true connection, friendship, and mutual respect. A love that felt safe, honest, and alive. Something Devin and I hadn't shared in a long time.

My body had grown tired of holding it all in. It became my truth-teller. I could no longer live the way I had been living and pretend it wasn't costing me. People had begun to wonder if I had cancer due to my rapid weight loss. As I continued to decline in energy and on the scale, I could feel something inside me shifting—an urgency to fight for me. My body had become the mirror I could no longer look away from.

— -

I decided to start counseling on my own. I told my therapist I was open to discussing anything—no topic off-limits—if it would help me feel better. We talked about my feelings for Anthony, my marriage, my family, and for the first time, my childhood abuse.

I had been on antidepressants for nearly a decade. But during this time, I made a decision that might sound reckless to some; I chose to go off of them. For once, I wanted to feel everything. The highs and the lows. The grief and the joy.

I started to think I was returning to myself.
   But the truth was more surprising: I was shedding old layers, meeting a version of me I'd never met. Waiting beneath the surface.

I'm not proud to admit that Anthony and I continued to wrestle with our feelings for a while. We met occasionally for lunch and messaged during the workday. Both of us were torn between love and loyalty, between what we felt and what we knew was right. But eventually, time and truth revealed what we couldn't yet face. It wasn't meant to be.

My heart broke all over again.

In the end, I lost my marriage to the man I gave my heart to for eighteen years and the best friend I thought was my soulmate. But out of the ashes, I gained freedom from a lifetime of emotional walls.

For the first time, my spirit felt free.
    It felt like a first breath. Unfamiliar, fragile, but undeniably mine.

PERSONAL INSIGHT

Sometimes the heart doesn't break, it reveals.

What felt like the destruction of everything familiar was really the shattering of the shell I had built to survive. The losses I endured—my marriage, a friendship I treasured, the fantasies I had clung to—became the cracks where truth finally slipped in.

Anthony wasn't meant to save me. The breaking point wasn't about a person. It was about the life I could no longer survive inside. He was the mirror that reflected how deeply I longed to be known, valued, healed and alive. That longing wasn't just about our connection, it was about the parts of me I abandoned in order to hold everything else together.

This wasn't a story of betrayal. It was the beginning of a metamorphosis. A slow, painful shedding of old expectations, old coping patterns, and old versions of myself. My heart didn't break to punish me. It broke to free me.

TAKEAWAYS

When your heart cracks open, it creates space for the truth you've been avoiding. Loss, no matter how devastating, often clears the ground for a deeper becoming. Grief is not just about what ends; it's about what is *unearthed* in the process.

You are not undone by heartbreak. You are uncovered by it. And in that uncovering lies the opportunity to choose yourself with a tenderness and honesty you may have never offered before.

Healing isn't about replacing what shattered. It's about discovering what was always waiting beneath the fractures.

SOUL NUGGETS

- *Some awakenings arrive disguised as endings.*
- *The heart cracks so the truth can get in.*
- *What falls apart releases the weight you were never meant to carry.*
- *The end of one story is often the beginning of your truest one.*

REFLECTION / JOURNAL PROMPTS

1. Who or what in your life has acted as a mirror, showing you parts of yourself you had buried or denied?

2. What emotions have you been numbing or avoiding, and what might they be trying to tell you?

3. Where in your life are you enduring something your body already knows is unsustainable??

4. How might you begin meeting yourself—your needs, desires, and truths—with the same tenderness you once offered others?

5. In what ways can heartbreak become an invitation to freedom?

YOUR VOICE

IS THE

light

THAT BREAKS THE

LONG-HELD

darkness.

#AThousandSmallResurrections

7

The Power of Truth Telling

With the crumbling of my marriage came the unraveling of a lifetime of secrets and traumas from my childhood. I committed myself to therapy and to the internal work my body had been begging for. It had finally reached its limit—my rapid weight loss was frightening. Years of suppressed thoughts, emotions, and memories had built up like pressure behind a dam beginning to crack.

That Sunday afternoon at my parents' house was one of the hardest thresholds I've ever crossed. For my whole life, I had tried to paint the picture of the perfect daughter, wife, and mother. Perfectionism had become my armor—shiny enough to distract, heavy enough to suffocate. Smile a little brighter. Look more put together. Work a little harder. Be the most creative. Host the grandest event. And maybe no one would notice how deeply I was unraveling inside.

The truth was, my marriage had endured painful blows, but I had kept the illusion of "fine" so intact that even I nearly believed it.

That day, I came alone to tell my dad and stepmom that my marriage was over, and that it wasn't what I had led them to believe. Sitting at the kitchen table, their shock was immediate. Their upset, expected. They insisted I was making a rash decision. I needed them to understand, so I began sharing the truth of what we had endured.

As I spoke, I watched their expressions soften. Their shoulders fell. Tears welled. And while their heartbreak deepened, something else was happening inside me: I felt a surge of power moving through me. All those years of silence had built up like pressure behind a dam beginning to crack—letting slivers of long-denied truth seep through. I began to feel lighter. Freer.

I told them I had been in therapy.
    And then I told them the secret I had carried for decades: that I had been sexually abused as a child by my stepdad.

I told them how it had shaped me, how it had haunted me. How I could no longer pretend it wasn't there.

What followed was a release—raw, holy, overdue. A purging of pain I had never allowed myself to name out loud. It felt like the weight of a truck had finally been lifted off my chest. What poured out wasn't just confession, it was resurrection. A part of me I thought had died stirred awake.

We cried. We held each other. We grieved together.

I left them broken that afternoon, but I walked away more whole than I had ever been.

That day changed everything. Silence had crippled me for too long, and I was finally done carrying what wasn't mine.

That day, a new Tammi emerged.

Empowered.

I had found my voice.

PERSONAL INSIGHT

Truth-telling was the moment my inner world shifted. When I finally spoke the words I had once swallowed, I wasn't simply releasing a secret, I was releasing the version of myself who had learned to live in the dark.

For years, silence had been my shield. It kept me functioning, kept the peace, kept the image intact. But silence also distorted me. It dimmed my light and blurred my reflection. I didn't realize how much of myself I had edited out just to maintain the illusion that everything was fine.

The day I spoke my truth aloud to my parents, something cracked open. Something ancient, something honest. I didn't crumble; **I emerged.**

The parts of me that had been buried beneath shame and fear finally rose to the surface, asking to be seen.

Truth didn't break me.

It reunited me with my soul.

TAKEAWAYS

Your truth is not too heavy, it's simply been carried in silence for longer than any heart was designed to endure. When you speak it out loud, you're not betraying anyone; you're unburdening yourself.

Truth-telling doesn't always lead to agreement, validation, or harmony. But it always leads to clarity. And clarity is the beginning of freedom.

When you choose honesty over image, you choose healing over hiding. You cannot step into your wholeness while shrinking yourself to protect the comfort, expectations, or denial of others.

Your truth is the doorway to your liberation.

SOUL NUGGETS

- *Silence may keep the peace, but it cannot keep you whole.*
- *Truth doesn't ruin what's real, it reveals it.*
- *The moment you speak, the walls you built to survive begin to fall.*

REFLECTION / JOURNAL PROMPTS

1. What truth in your life has been whispering for years, waiting for permission to be spoken?

2. How has keeping quiet protected you, and how has it cost you?

3. When you imagine speaking your truth, what shift do you feel in your body?

4. What comfort have you been prioritizing over your own healing, and why?

5. If you laid down the burden of secrecy, who might you finally become?

WHEN YOU CAN

speak

TO WHAT CHASED

YOU, IT CAN

no longer

HAUNT YOU.

#AThousandSmallResurrections

8

Facing the Faceless Man

Once you find your voice, it's nearly impossible to go backward.

For me, it felt like the forward momentum of a rollercoaster. Healing had been the slow, steady tick upward—intentional, terrifying, necessary. But once I reached the top, the drop was fast, fierce, and liberating.

I was no longer bracing for impact with my eyes shut. I was wide-eyed, hands lifted, screaming through the wind—alive. The adrenaline of reclaiming my voice and power pushed me toward something I never thought I would do.

One afternoon, with my heart pounding, I picked up the phone and called my ex-stepdad.

Another version of me rose up in that moment. Strong, steady, and unapologetically clear. My inner child needed this. My grown woman self needed this. My soul needed this. For every moment I had been frozen in fear, silenced by shame, unable to speak—I needed to finally say the words I couldn't back then.

I gave voice to the memories he created, the confusion he caused, the pain he left behind.

I explained how excruciating it had been to rebuild myself from what he stole.

I wanted him to hear it.
   To feel the weight of it.
   To know that I remembered.

Reliving it was painful, but necessary. I wasn't calling for his apology. I wasn't calling for understanding. I wasn't calling for reconciliation.

I was calling for freedom.

This time, **I held the power.**

His voice trembled when he said, "I'm sorry."

And I believe he meant it.

But I didn't need it. His remorse couldn't rewrite the past. What mattered was that I had spoken—that the truth had finally left my body.

And that's exactly what I needed most.

I haven't had the nightmare of the faceless man since.

PERSONAL INSIGHT

Speaking to him was never about what he would say, it was about who I finally allowed myself to become. Finding my voice showed me that I wasn't seeking closure from someone else; I was reclaiming the part of me that had been silenced for years. That phone call wasn't about his apology. It was about releasing the truth my body had carried for too long. In naming what he'd took, I took myself back. The nightmare didn't end because he spoke, it ended because *I finally did.*

TAKEAWAY

Your healing doesn't depend on someone else acknowledging what they did. It begins the moment you choose to give your truth a voice. When you confront the places that once terrified you, the shadows lose their power. Freedom arrives not when someone releases you, but when you release yourself.

SOUL NUGGETS

- *Your courage is louder than your fear.*
- *What once silenced you now strengthens you.*
- *You don't need permission to heal.*

REFLECTION / JOURNAL PROMPTS

1. What conversation—external or internal—could bring you closer to closure?

2. What fear keeps you from speaking your truth to the person, memory, or moment that hurt you?

3. If your healed self could speak to your wounded self, what would she say?

4. What would it look like to reclaim your power from the past today?

5. Is there a "faceless man" in your story; someone or something you still avoid confronting? Why?

67

BECOMING *yourself* IS THE *bravest* LEAP YOU'LL EVER TAKE.

#AThousandSmallResurrections

9

When the Sky Opens

Now divorced and a single mom of two teenagers, I stepped into a new era of self-discovery. For the first time, I was living on my own and learning who I was outside of marriage, outside of motherhood, and outside of anything I'd ever been told to be.

In my free time, I started yoga, took belly-dance classes, and discovered a passion for cooking. I became curious about wine pairings, sushi, and how to grill my own perfect steak. I took my kids camping and on a weekend adventure to Duluth, MN.

I fell in love with biking and bought myself a fancy street bike for long rides. Eventually leading me into bike racing. I decorated my home, took myself to the movies, treated myself to solo dinners, and spent many Friday nights wandering the bookstore, curled up in a cozy chair with a stack of books. Oh, how I love the smell and quiet adventure of a bookstore. It has always been one of my happy places.

I even dared skydiving!

Skydiving, I realized, is a lot like life: scary as hell, breathtakingly beautiful, and completely dependent on your willingness to trust the jump. You can't experience the expansive view unless you're willing to let go.

Life felt good. I was content being single—but companionship still tugged at my heart.

— -

Taking the Leap

At my girlfriend's urging, I joined a dating website. I had no idea what I was doing—after all, I'd been in relationships since eighth grade and married at nineteen. Dating in my thirties felt like a foreign language.

Most dates were duds. Some were creepy. Finding a man without baggage seemed nearly impossible.

Just as I was ready to give up, a new message appeared in my inbox.

— -

The Beginning of Us

Keith lived slightly outside my search range, but distance didn't stop us. We started chatting, and for the first time, I felt a genuine connection.

This man was charming, handsome, emotionally open, seemingly stable, and attentive in ways the others hadn't been. Our first date turned into a weekend of golf, great food, and deep conversation. I loved that he spoke openly and emotionally about his childhood, his foster siblings, and the people he loved. I admired a man who wore his heart on his sleeve.

We bonded over DIY home projects, biking, golf, and quiet weekends together. There were some red flags in the early stages of our dating, but I brushed them aside.

He moved quickly—faster than I was fully ready for—but I went along because it felt exciting and new. He had me meeting his family and spending time with his son just weeks after we started seeing each other. When I expressed my concern and shared that my heart was guarded, he promised I could trust him. And slowly, I did.

One weekend while doing home renovations, I overheard him arguing intensely with his dad in the other room over something seemingly trivial. It was jarring—completely out of character—and quite unsettling. Despite my shock, I told myself it must've been an isolated outburst.

But the real concern I had was his relationship with his son's mother.

Their interactions and enmeshment often crossed boundaries. When I expressed my discomfort and the confusion it could create for their son, I was met with defensiveness or told I was overreacting. Eventually, I began to doubt myself. Maybe I was being too sensitive. Maybe my past trauma was clouding my judgment.

So I silenced the voice inside me.

Over the next two years, my unease grew. Twice I ended things. Twice he begged me back with promises of change. He was persistent. After our final breakup, he said he had implemented better boundaries, was ready to commit, and wanted a life with me. We reconciled.

Not long after, he proposed, moved into my place, and I began planning the wedding of my dreams.

I was hopeful again.

—-

Dreams and Detours

After we married, we dreamed of expanding our family. Although I hadn't planned on more children at this stage of my life, agreeing to try felt like reclaiming something I hadn't realized I'd lost.

Four months after our wedding, I was pregnant.

Life became a whirlwind—five of us in my townhome, with a sixth on the way. We needed something bigger, but the housing market had crashed and neither of our places were selling. To make matters worse, I got laid off from my job. Managing three mortgages would've been impossible. So my husband chose to turn his home into rental property and encouraged me to default on mine, promising he'd take care of us.

I hesitated.
    I was anxious.
    I had worked so hard after my divorce to build my life, my credit, and my stability.

But again, I silenced my instincts and agreed.

PERSONAL INSIGHT

I was discovering identity, joy, curiosity, and strength, but the past patterns of self-betrayal still lived quietly beneath the surface. Even in this era of expansion, I hadn't fully learned to honor the voice within me. These moments were the seeds of the lesson to come: that the woman I had found was real, even if the next chapter would test her.

TAKEAWAY

New eras teach us who we are without anyone else's voice drowning us out. But they also reveal the places where we still override our intuition in the name of love, hope, or belonging. Growth isn't a single smooth rise. It's a series of leaps, stumbles, pivots, and awakenings.

SOUL NUGGETS

- *Your joy is your birthright, not a phase.*
- *Intuition whispers long before it screams.*
- *Becoming yourself requires choosing yourself again and again.*

REFLECTION / JOURNAL PROMPTS

1. What activities, spaces, or hobbies make you feel most like yourself?

2. When have you silenced your intuition for the sake of connection, peace, or hope?

3. What "red flags" have you excused because you didn't want to start over?

4. How do you know, in your body, when your intuition is speaking?

75

SOMETIMES PAIN

reflects

BACK TO US

SO WE CAN

FINALLY SEE IT

clearly.

#AThousandSmallResurrections

10

Mirrored Wounds

It was a Friday afternoon. The day before my sister's wedding. We were packing for a weekend of festivities while my husband was locked in a heated text exchange with his ex over custody of my stepson.

Tension filled the room.
  Tension filled my body.

Frustrated with the delay and the emotional chaos, I demanded to see his phone.

And there it was.

In her rage—and in attempt to get her way—she threatened to expose everything to me. She sent him a message detailing romantic encounters they'd had during our dating and engagement. She listed specifics. Proof that was impossible to deny.

He had no words.

Standing in my walk-in closet, the air left my lungs. My world collapsed inward. The truth of my suspicions were staring me in the face.

Everything I had questioned countless times was suddenly, painfully confirmed.

And I was six months pregnant.
Unemployed.
My credit ruined.
My trust shattered.

I was living the same nightmare, *twice.*

But I couldn't fall apart—not yet. I had to put on my dress, smile for photos, and stand beside my sister as her maid of honor. I swallowed pain, held my tears, and somehow got through the weekend.

When I returned home, I stared at my reflection in the mirror—swollen eyes, broken heart, and a spirit barely holding itself together.

I told myself I had survived this before. I could do it again.

There had to be a reason this pain had been delivered twice.
There had to be something I wasn't seeing.
Something I needed to learn.

I didn't want another divorce. I didn't want my stepson or unborn baby to experience the struggle my older kids had lived through. What I had also gone through as a child.

The fact was: I didn't have a job, my credit was ruined, and I had no safety net to fall back on.

So I promised myself I would rise above it.

I would try to rebuild.

I would fight for the family I thought we could be.

PERSONAL INSIGHT

When the truth surfaced, it didn't just expose his betrayal, it revealed how deeply I had been abandoning myself. In that moment, despite how crushed I felt, I wasn't being punished; I was being redirected. The pain forced me to face the patterns I kept repeating and the moments where I silenced the very intuition trying to protect me. That moment wasn't my breaking. It was my unveiling. As harsh as it was, the truth became the beginning of me choosing myself in a way I never had before.

TAKEAWAYS

Truth may shatter your illusion, but it will never shatter you. When clarity arrives—no matter how painful—it shows you where you've been settling, shrinking, or carrying someone else's deception. Betrayal doesn't define your worth; it illuminates where honesty is needed for your direction, your boundaries, your healing, and your freedom. Sometimes the truth feels like loss, but it's actually the doorway back to yourself.

SOUL NUGGETS

- *A broken heart is not a broken woman.*
- *God will interrupt your illusion before He lets you lose yourself.*
- *Clarity hurts, but it also heals.*

REFLECTION / JOURNAL PROMPTS

1. What truth have you been avoiding because of what it might cost you?

2. When your intuition is confirmed, do you trust yourself, or do you doubt yourself?

3. Where in your life do you need clarity, even if it scares you?

4. What patterns keep repeating in your relationships, and what might they be trying to reveal?

rebuilding
AFTER TRAUMA
IS
courageous,
EVEN WHEN IT
FEELS FRAGILE.

#AThousandSmallResurrections

11

Cracks In the Foundation

Rebuilding after betrayal is a strange kind of hope.

It's not the buoyant hope that comes with beginnings, but the trembling kind that rises after survival.

I told myself I could do it again. I had rebuilt once before.

So I began piecing together a new version of life—painting over cracks, patching what I could, pretending the foundation wasn't broken.

There were good moments, of course. Enough to convince me that maybe, eventually, things would be okay.

We welcomed our baby.
   We found a new home in a beautiful neighborhood.
   Life looked whole from the outside.

But beneath the surface, something was shifting.

I wasn't the same woman who rebuilt after divorce. This time, I was hardened. Guarded. Carrying scars I tried to ignore.

Anger lingered—not just at him, but at myself.
    For trusting.
    For believing.
    For wanting so badly to make it work that I lost sight of my own truth.

He said he wanted to make things right. He took some accountability. But remorse never rooted. Apologies were often tools for moving past discomfort, not catalysts for change.

Counseling didn't last. Resolution never came.

And yet, he expected healing to be linear—tidy, quick, and convenient.

"Can't you just move on?"

But healing doesn't happen on demand. It doesn't happen through pressure. It happens through presence.

Eventually, it became easier not to talk about it at all. So I buried the wound and called it forgiveness. I fell back into believing silence meant strength. That swallowing pain meant peace.

But unspoken pain never disappears. It festers. And I knew that.

In burying it, I became disconnected.
    From him.
    From myself.
    From my spirit.

The truth I didn't want to face was this:

What I convinced myself was rebuilding, was actually the beginning of my unraveling.

The betrayal didn't just break my trust, it weakened the foundation beneath us. And instead of becoming stronger, I slowly began to disappear.

What looked like rebuilding from the outside was, on the inside, the quiet beginning of losing myself to an all-to-familiar pattern.

PERSONAL INSIGHT

Rebuilding after betrayal felt like I was walking on a tightrope—hope in one hand, fear in the other. I wanted so badly to forgive, to restore, to redeem the story but the effort slowly eroded my confidence and dimmed my light. I see now that true resilience isn't just about surviving the fallout, it's about recognizing the erosion, naming it, and choosing to reclaim yourself piece by piece.

Our relationship was never truly repaired; it had simply been covered. And what isn't healed doesn't disappear. It waits.

TAKEAWAYS

Erosion is subtle until it isn't. Acknowledge the small cracks before they widen. Denying them delays healing; naming them opens the door to clarity. Remember: forgiveness is about freedom, not returning to the place where you lost yourself.

Small, intentional acts such as prayer, journaling, breathing, space, grounding in truth, help you re-anchor in your identity. Healing begins with honesty, not endurance.

SOUL NUGGETS

- *Betrayal doesn't define your value or your future.*
- *Silence isn't strength, truth is.*
- *Hope after betrayal is trembling, not perfect, and that's enough.*
- *You are allowed to choose yourself, even when it means walking away.*

REFLECTION / JOURNAL PROMPTS

1. When have you stayed in a situation hoping to restore it, even when it was hurting you?

2. Can you recall a time when hope felt fragile, yet you chose to move forward anyway? What helped you?

3. What small act could you take today to honor your boundaries or your worth?

87

4. Who or what has helped you validate your experience and remind you of your value?

YOUR

worth

IS NOT DEFINED

BY HOW

OTHERS TREAT

you.

#AThousandSmallResurrections

12

The Erosion of Self

By the time I realized we weren't truly rebuilding, the damage had already begun. What followed wasn't sudden or explosive—it was slow, subtle, and devastating in ways I couldn't name at the time.

Little comments he spoke that made me doubt myself.
Sharp words that cut at my spirit.
Silent treatments that felt like punishment.
Apologies that soothed the moment but didn't change the pattern.

Slowly, I began to shrink.
My light dimmed.
My confidence cracked.

I was being conditioned—taught to question my own reality.

This wasn't rebuilding.
This was erosion.

Emptiness replaced hope. Anger replaced patience. And eventually, what I once called love became the very thing that chipped away at me, one small piece at a time, until I scarcely recognized the woman in the mirror.

He took my scars—my wounds and insecurities—and began using them as ammunition. It wasn't always loud. Sometimes it was just a tone, a look, a backhanded comment. But when he was angry, his words could slice straight through me.

Not just me, but our kids too.

I became hyper-protective. I fought often. Fire with fire. But the constant fighting and screaming wasn't healthy. The tension in our home seeped into everyone.

I wasn't protecting us from physical danger, but from emotional and verbal blows.

Things like,

"Oh, Tammi had to go and find her voice. I'm so sick of it."

Or, "Of course, I get stuck dealing with all the baggage Devin left you with. You've 'found your voice,' remember?"

For years, in my first marriage, we rarely fought. I used to retreat, stay silent, and keep the peace. But my healing journey had taught me to speak up, and now I was being punished for it.

He was skilled at pushing me to my breaking point and then using my reaction against me.

"See? You're the crazy one," he'd say.

Everything became:
 "That's your problem."

I often found myself saying aloud, "I don't like who I am when I'm with you."
 This relationship had carved out a version of me I didn't recognize: hardened, defensive, bitter.

My body lived in a constant state of vigilance. Fight or flight. I never knew which version of him would walk through the door. I was always bracing.

As the months turned to years, the erosion didn't roar—it whispered. It slipped in through the smallest cracks.

My confidence began to slide.
 Decisions started to feel impossible.
 Even choosing what to make for dinner felt like a risk.

I had survived so much in my life, but this... this broke me differently.
 It made me doubt me.

I clung to anything that lifted my spirit—prayer, journaling, bible studies, girls' nights, affirmations, vision boards. Anything to keep my light from being snuffed out.

But whenever I tried to do anything for myself, he'd complain. When I stayed home, I felt invisible. Like I was a fixture meant to clean, cook, manage schedules, pay bills, keep everything moving. Yet even then, I couldn't do that right in his eyes.

If I was so bad, I'd ask, "Why did you even marry me?"

He found ways to silence my voice. My spirit.
   "You go on, and on, and on, and on!"
   "What you say brings no value to a conversation."

In public he praised me.
   At home, those same qualities became my flaws.

It was emotional whiplash.

No amount of self-lifting could offset the nightly collapse of my spirit.

Our boys began treating me the way they saw him treat me. And nothing pierced me deeper than realizing they might think this was what love looked like... or that they might carry it into their own relationships someday.

When I returned to therapy to process resurfacing trauma and the weight of our family's struggles, I could finally see how completely I had lost myself in this relationship.

Our kids were hurting too.

Our youngest began struggling with severe anxiety and depression, often breaking down or lashing out when arguments escalated. We created a code word he could use when he felt overwhelmed. A signal for me to try to de-escalate.
   My stepson responded differently. He retreated. Hid. Shut down.

Both were hurting in ways words couldn't capture.

The heaviness in our home was suffocating.

My body began to break under the weight of it all—debilitating sciatica, shoulder pain, carpal tunnel, chest pain, constant illness. The stress was manifesting, just like before.

We were broke, emotionally and financially. On the outside, it looked like we had it all together. On the inside, we were falling apart. The resentment grew. Respect faded.

We weren't even hiding our fights in public anymore.

Then one day, in a fog of self-doubt, I stumbled across an article about narcissism. Every word felt like it was written for me. Like someone had captured my story, my home, my heartbreak, my confusion.

I felt seen. Validated.
   I wasn't imagining it.
   I wasn't overreacting.
   I wasn't "too much."

What I was living had a name.

Love bombing.
   Control.
   Devaluation.
   Reversal.
   The rewrite.

It was a quiet but powerful awakening.

I began rebuilding myself and my spirit behind the scenes.

Then one day, he announced we needed to sell the house. He had been in and out of jobs. I struggled to find full-time work. Our finances were a mess.

I begged to find another way, but his mind was made up.

Somewhere in that fog, a small truth began to whisper. It didn't come all at once. Instead, it came in moments:
A quiet truth in reflection.
A comment from a friend.
The sound of my child's trembling voice.
A revelation during therapy.
Validation from a family member.

And then one day, as I sat alone in a room I no longer felt safe in, the truth surfaced:
I could leave.
I could choose something different.
I wasn't trapped.
I wasn't powerless.
I didn't have to stay in the version of myself this relationship had sculpted.

That realization wasn't loud or triumphant—it was trembling, fragile, almost sacred. But it was *mine*. And it was enough.

So while I packed boxes, I quietly looked for an attorney and a place of my own.

Leaving wasn't an act of anger.
  It was an act of love.
  For myself.
  for my children,
  and in a strange way, even for him.

Our brokenness had become louder than our intentions.

PERSONAL INSIGHT

Looking back, I can see how quietly and completely I disappeared beneath someone else's version of me. The erosion didn't happen overnight. It happened in the small silences, the tearing down of my self worth, the belief that I wasn't good enough. Naming the patterns, understanding the cycle, and finally recognizing myself in the pages of an article wasn't just information, it was validation. It reminded me I wasn't broken; I had been broken down. That truth became the foundation of my healing. It helped me remember who I was, and eventually, it gave me the strength to choose myself again.

Today, I am more grounded, more peaceful, more healthy, and more aligned with who I truly am than I ever was within that storm.

And I'm committed to showing my kids what a peaceful home looks like. How kindness sounds. How safety feels. How words matter. How differing perspectives don't have to turn into battles.

How love should feel safe.

TAKEAWAYS

Emotional abuse often begins subtly, slowly eroding your confidence and sense of self. Recognizing the patterns is the first step toward protecting your boundaries and reclaiming your life.

Healing isn't about forcing reconciliation; it's about creating space for your own peace, clarity and growth.

Validation, even from unexpected places, can ignite courage and change.

Protecting your children includes modeling what a healthy, safe, and respectful environment looks like. Breaking generational cycles.

SOUL NUGGETS

- *Healing is not linear; you are allowed to move at your own pace.*
- *Recognizing patterns is the first step to reclaiming your power.*
- *Leaving isn't failure, it's an act of courage and self-love.*
- *Rebuilding can be done quietly, patiently, and on your own terms.*

REFLECTION / JOURNAL PROMPTS

1. When have you stayed in a relationship or situation hoping to fix it, even at the expense of your own well-being? What did that cost you?

2. Can you recall subtle moments when your confidence or sense of self was diminished? How did it make you feel?

3. Have you ever experienced a moment of validation that helped you see your reality more clearly? How did it impact your healing?

4. What small actions could you take today to reclaim your energy, boundaries, or your voice?

5. How can understanding your past help you make healthier relationship choices moving forward?

** If this story struck something in you, resources for support and healing are available at the back of this book. Help is one of the ways God meets us in our need.*

PEACE IS NOT
THE ABSENCE OF
fear,
BUT THE
PRESENCE OF
spirit IN IT.

#AThousandSmallResurrections

13

Broken Open

What started out as a routine physical took a sharp turn when the new physician asked, "How long have you had your heart murmur?"

"What heart murmur?" I replied.

"You've never been told you have one?" he asked, surprised.

"No," I answered.

"Well, it's likely nothing," he said, "but just to be sure, I'm going to recommend you see a cardiologist."

I left fairly unfazed, but a few days later I made the appointment.

I remember sitting in the waiting area of the heart institute, scanning the room and thinking I didn't belong there. I was forty-two and in decent shape. Most of the people around me were significantly older or heavier. I felt annoyed—convinced this was a waste of my time—but figured I'd be in and out quickly. Just another box checked off my to-do list.

After reviewing my echocardiogram, the young, eager doctor walked in looking almost excited, as though he had just discovered something rare. Without hesitation he said, "You've got a bicuspid aortic valve! You'll most likely need heart surgery at some point."

I just stared at him, dumbfounded.

"Not now. But sometime down the road." he clarified.

"You were born with a congenital heart defect. Over time, this can cause the valve to break down faster. Yours is already showing moderate deterioration. We'll need to monitor it annually, and when it reaches a severe level, surgery will be required."

And there it was—the diagnosis I never expected.

I walked out in disbelief. Heart surgery? At my age? I had a toddler at home. I worked out three to four times a week, ate healthy, biked, and ran 5Ks. How could I have a heart problem when I felt fine? And how had this never been detected before?

My husband urged me to get a second opinion, and I brought him along this time to ask the questions I couldn't when my brain was in shock. The second cardiologist agreed with the first diagnosis, but reassured us it could be years before things progressed. "Go home," he said, "and don't let this weigh on you."

So I brushed it off as best I could and carried on.

At my first annual checkup a year later, I went alone again. Nothing much had changed… or so I thought. After the echo, the same energetic doctor walked in with a different tone.

"Well," he said, "it's time."

"Time for what?" I asked.

"Your valve is leaking and regurgitating at a severe level now. I know a great surgeon I think you should meet with."

There it was again, another diagnosis I didn't see coming. Everything he said afterward became muffled background noise against the voice in my head: *This can't be real.*

At least this time, I had the presence of mind to ask for everything in writing, knowing I wouldn't remember it otherwise.

The surgeon confirmed the diagnosis, but what shook me even more was when he showed us a video of my enlarged heart. "You're in acute heart failure," he said. "Without surgery, you likely won't survive a year."

This wasn't optional. So we scheduled surgery for early January, after the holidays.

I had six weeks to prepare. I read books, created a health care directive, joined an online community of heart valve patients, and tried to brace myself. But my health declined quickly. My arms and legs went numb from lack of blood flow. I grew light-headed, exhausted, and needed to rest constantly.

We gently told our kids, family, and friends. I tried to stay positive for them, but in the quiet hours of the night, I couldn't hold back the anxious thoughts and my fearful heart. I listened to a playlist of songs on repeat, prayed, and wept. I pleaded with God for more time. I had so much more I wanted to see, do, and experience.

Nothing changes you more than being faced with your own mortality.

While surgery and recovery were physically grueling, it was the mental battle beforehand—the fear, the loneliness, the wrestling with faith— that felt even harder.

But in those dark and lonely moments, God met me where I was. I can't explain it, but one night, through tears and on my knees, I whispered, "Please God, give me peace no matter what Your will is for me." And instantly, a wave of calm washed over me—deep into my soul. When I prayed for comfort, I felt peace and warmth surround me like the softest, coziest blanket.

He had answered my prayer.

The surgery went perfectly. My failing valve was replaced, and my heart returned to normal size and function within hours of beating on its own again. I spent ten days in the hospital regaining strength and adjusting to the blood thinners I'd take for life. The surgeon assured me that the St. Jude mechanical valve stitched into my heart was built to last.

And in that hospital bed—with tubes, pain, and the slow expanding of breath—something in me quietly rose again. A small resurrection. One of many I didn't yet realize life had in store.

PERSONAL INSIGHT

I had spent years powering through life. Strong, capable, and constantly holding everything together. But facing my own mortality stripped me down to what was undeniably true: I am not in control.

This diagnosis forced me to confront the limits of my strength and the illusion that I could outrun fear, pain, or vulnerability. What I once saw as chaos or catastrophe became the very place God met me. Not in my striving, but in my surrender.

The fear of dying didn't take me away from myself; it brought me home to a deeper trust, a softer strength, and a peace I couldn't manufacture on my own. Looking back, that season wasn't just a crisis. It was one of my thousand small resurrections. The places where something in me had to break open so something truer could rise.

TAKEAWAYS

Our bodies often reveal what our souls have been trying to say: that something within us needs attention, care, and gentleness.

Peace doesn't always come when things get better; often, it comes when we stop fighting what is and rest in God's presence.

God doesn't waste pain. Even the messiest, scariest chapters can become sacred ground for transformation.

Healing begins when we stop pretending we're fine and allow ourselves to be fully seen, known, and held by God and by others.

Every moment we face what we fear, and choose truth over pretending, is a kind of resurrection.

SOUL NUGGETS

- *Sometimes God lets what is fragile break so He can rebuild what is eternal.*
- *Your body often tells the truth before your mind is willing to listen.*
- *Surrender isn't giving up, it's opening up to what can finally heal you.*
- *Every time your spirit rises after being shaken, that too is resurrection.*

REFLECTION / JOURNAL PROMPTS

1.. Have you ever received news that stopped you in your tracks—a diagnosis, loss, or change that made life feel suddenly fragile?

2.. How do you typically respond to fear or uncertainty? By fighting, fleeing, numbing, or surrendering?

3.. Can you recall a time when God's peace met you in the middle of the storm, not by changing your circumstances, but by changing your heart?

4.. What role does gratitude play when life feels unfair or overwhelming?

5.. Where in your life can you recognize a "small resurrection"? A moment when something within you rose again after breaking open?

II

The Reflection

At some point, you stop running from the glass.
You look into it—back at what was,
inward at what is, and forward with eyes finally open.
This is where clarity begins.

healing
IS NOT JUST
SURVIVAL, IT IS
remembering
WHY YOU'RE
STILL HERE.

#AThousandSmallResurrections

14

Made For More

The Heart of My Awakening

Leaving the hospital was emotional. Gratitude overwhelmed me as I walked the halls one last time. With tears in my eyes, I thanked the staff who had cared for me. But it was the drive home that truly broke me open.

The moment I got into the car, the song *Word of God Speak*—one I had played on repeat before surgery—came on the radio. I don't believe in coincidences.

That song had carried me through nights when fear was louder than faith. It reminded me that sometimes the most powerful answer from God isn't a miracle, it's His presence..

Tears poured down my face. My God had been with me in the dark and gave me peace when I had begged for it, carried me through the pain, and handed me a second chance at life. He had never left my side. Not for a moment.

And then I heard a voice clearly say: **You were never meant to coast. You were made for more. I have so much more for you.**

In a flash, I was brought back to a moment months before my diagnosis…

Depressed and disconnected, I had been sitting on the couch reflecting while my youngest napped. My marriage was strained. We fought constantly. I felt numb to passion, purpose, and joy. On the outside, I had a beautiful life—our home, our friends, our children—but inside I felt empty.

I remember looking around my space and thinking, *Most people would love the life I have.* Frustrated with myself, I whispered out loud, "Tammi, for God's sake, suck it up."

And in that moment, I decided I would just "coast" from here on out. I had always been in search for more and I was done. I was throwing in the towel. I told myself I should be content with what I had. It was good enough.

But as we drove home from the hospital that day, it was like God was gently shaking His head and saying: **There was never going to be any coasting My beautiful child. You've got a purpose here. You were made for more.**

My recovery wasn't smooth.

Just a week after returning home, I was readmitted with Pericarditis— inflammation of the heart lining. If I thought open-heart surgery was painful, this was something else. Fluid buildup suffocates the heart from the inside, and the pain was excruciating. The procedure to drain it required a massive needle be inserted while awake which was no cake walk either.

For months afterward, I lived with chronic Pericarditis, requiring heavy medication. It felt like walking around with a mild heart attack every day. To make things worse, my sternum wasn't healing properly. The rib they severed to reach my valve wouldn't fuse back. Every movement caused my rib to shift painfully out of place.

For nine months, I slept propped up on the couch, waking in tears and screaming out in pain if I accidentally rolled over.

Finally, a year later, I agreed to another surgery to insert a titanium plate to stabilize my sternum. It worked.

Now, eleven years later, the physical scars and the quiet ticking of my mechanical valve are constant reminders of God's goodness and the gift of every breath. I still have occasional flare-ups of Pericarditis and chest sensitivity, but I am thriving.

I am no longer coasting. I am living each day with intention like someone who's been given her life back and refuses to waste it.

— -

When life breaks us open, it also gives us a chance to see what's been hidden inside. The strength, purpose, and faith that were always there but buried beneath the noise of doing and surviving.

My diagnosis didn't just change my body; it transformed the way I saw life itself. Every heartbeat became a reminder that I am still here, still becoming, still called to live with intention.

God didn't just repair my heart—**He reawakened it.**

The very pain I prayed away became the doorway to a deeper peace, and the quiet ticking inside my chest now keeps rhythm with a truth I can no longer ignore: **there is beauty in the breaking, grace in the waiting, and joy—even here—in the sacred mess of being made new.**

And perhaps that's the essence of every resurrection: not one dramatic moment, but a thousand quiet, ordinary awakenings that pull us back to life again.

PERSONAL INSIGHT

My awakening didn't arrive in a single moment, it unfolded slowly, through fear, surrender, pain, and grace. Held together by stitches and prayer, I realized how much of my life I had spent surviving instead of truly living. I had convinced myself that "coasting" was safer than wanting more, safer than risking disappointment, safer than admitting how unhappy and disconnected I really was.

But God used the breaking of my physical heart to expose a deeper truth:

I was never created to live small, quiet, or numb. His whisper on that drive home was not about ambition. It was about purpose, intention, and spiritual rebirth. About remembering who I was before life made me settle.

This chapter of my life didn't just save my heart; **it revived my spirit.**

TAKEAWAYS

Purpose often emerges from pain; the places where we crack open are often where God breathes new life into us.

When we surrender control, we create space for divine redirection. Sometimes, the "new path" is the truer one we avoided for years.

Gratitude turns ordinary moments into sacred encounters and anchors us in what is real, steady, and eternal.

You are not defined by what happened to you, but by how you rise, heal, and choose to love again.

You were never meant to "coast." You were created to live with intention, courage, and soul-deep purpose.

SOUL NUGGETS

- *When God says you were made for more, He means more peace, more purpose, more life, not more striving.*
- *Awakening often begins in the places you thought would break you.*

- *Sometimes God rebuilds what we resisted letting fall apart.*
- *Even the smallest whisper from God can resurrect what fear tried to bury.*

REFLECTION / JOURNAL PROMPTS

1. When was the last time you sensed God whispering that you were made for more even when life had convinced you to "coast"?

2. How has facing your own limitations or mortality shifted your priorities or deepened your faith?

3. In what ways has God used your pain or setbacks to point you back to purpose?

4. How do you now define "living fully"? What does it look like in this season of your life?

5. Who or what helps you stay attuned to the still, small voice of God in your everyday rhythms of life?

115

vulnerability

IS THE

DOORWAY

TO

connection.

#AThousandSmallResurrections

15

The Courage to be Seen

After my heart surgery, I began to see life differently and through new eyes. I felt a deep pull to live with more intention. Much of my time was spent simply being present, soaking in the moment, letting life touch me in a way I had never allowed before. I also began to reflect more deeply on my purpose; the reason I'd been given a second chance at life.

When I returned home from the hospital, I distinctly heard these words rise within me:

You weren't made to settle. There's still so much more for you.

The call on my heart was clear: I was meant to help others—specifically women. To help them unlock their voices. To share their stories. To tell their truth boldly and without apology.

I had learned firsthand that keeping quiet keeps us small—unhealed and disconnected from the fullness of who we were created to be. Silence distances us from authenticity; from ourselves, and from the version of us we present to the world.

The truth is, we are all flawed and broken humans, walking around with many of the same fears and insecurities. Yet we pretend we're the only ones who feel this way—that no one else would understand.

But when we hide portions of who we are, we stay disconnected. I've learned that the more open I've been about my life, the more others have opened up to me. We discover how much we truly have in common and how much healing can happen when we share. Sometimes, a listening ear is all it takes to help someone make it through the day.

True connection brings shared resources, new perspectives, moral support, emotional healing, and even physical healing.

— -

One day, I decided to launch a little social media experiment called **"Just Keeping It Real."** It was meant to be a lighthearted way to spark honest conversation about the things we don't normally post online. Like a photo with no makeup, a hidden insecurity, a quirky talent, or a memory (happy or hard) we rarely share.

The goal was simple: connect people, create community, live more authentically, and spark a revolution of confident, healed truth-tellers.

While the experiment didn't take off quite like I hoped, it did something else just as important—it pushed me to boldly step into my own truth.

I chose to get vulnerable and share a piece of my childhood abuse story.

I posted a picture of myself at ten years old and wrote about her: about her laugh, her innocence, her free spirit, and how all of that was taken advantage of and manipulated. How it changed her.

It was bold. It was terrifying. Hitting "post" felt like jumping off a cliff. For a split second, I regretted it.

But then the comments and private messages began pouring in. Messages of love, pride, and courage. People thanked me for sharing, confiding that it had happened to them too. They said my words brought them peace, connection, validation, even healing.

Walls became bridges.

Some reached out privately with their own stories. Expressing that my courage had given them permission to finally speak their truth. It was an unfortunate bond, yet one that connected us deeply.

What I learned was:
   Sharing heals you, but it also heals others. Your journey might be someone else's roadmap. Your test might be someone else's testimony.

You matter.
   Your story matters.
   Your voice is needed.

PERSONAL INSIGHT

I often wonder, *What if it's meant to be a dance?* A rhythmic dance of connection to each other. Not a perfect image of what we project of ourselves or our lives out into the world, but a blend of the good *and* the hard.

What if we woke up to realize we've all been going about it wrong? Instead of living only parts of ourselves out loud, what if we allowed it to became normal to share the pieces of us we deem imperfect, flawed or broken? What if *that* is what's necessary to soften hearts, maybe soften the world?

The truth is, we are all the same. Each one of us trying to hide the same big secret: that we are broken and imperfect. We're all living with the same belief that being imperfect is somehow unique only to us. But imagine if everyone could recognize that none of us have it all figured out. We are all in-process, navigating life, and learning how to heal and grow. Maybe then, we could relax into our most authentic selves.

Because our brokenness—our humanness—is actually what connects us.

TAKEAWAYS

Your story carries power. Far more than you realize. When you speak your truth, even in small, gentle ways, you open the door for others to step into theirs. Your vulnerability becomes someone else's permission slip.

Healing is rarely a solo journey; it is something we build together by showing up as our honest selves.

The parts of you that you think will push others away are often the very parts that draw them closer.

There is someone out there who needs exactly what you carry.

SOUL NUGGETS

- *Your truth is a bridge, not a burden.*
- *Connection begins where pretending ends.*
- *Your story is medicine. Someone is waiting for the dose only you can give.*
- *Healing expands when shared.*

REFLECTION / JOURNAL PROMPTS

1. What part of your story have you been afraid to share, and why?

2. When has someone else's vulnerability helped you feel seen, under-stood, or less alone?

3. If you could whisper one truth to your younger self, what would it be?

4. What would authentic connection look like in your life right now?

122

5. Where can you take one small step toward speaking your truth with yourself or with someone you trust?

WE WEATHER
THE STORMS
best
WHEN WE REFUSE
TO LET GO OF ONE
another.

#AThousandSmallResurrections

16

Held Through the Storm

The sacredness of our human experience lies not only in the moments we celebrate but in the ones we survive together. And sometimes, the deepest lessons don't come from our own suffering—they come from standing in the fire with someone we love.

Not all of our pain is personal.

Friends or family navigating life altering diagnoses or chronic illness. Job loss. Struggling marriages. The quiet ache of watching a parent or grandparent fade from Cancer, Dementia or Alzheimer's. Supporting someone through child loss, addiction, eating disorders, depression, anxiety. Or simply trying to raise children in a world that feels increasingly heavy.

Life's hardships are real, normal and expected. Yet we are never truly prepared for how they take us down, take hold of us, or shape our lives—sometimes temporarily, sometimes permanently.

We all wear our struggles differently.

Some of my hardest moments have come from watching people I love suffer. I've always taken on others' pain as if it were my own—an instinct that traces back to childhood, when carrying what wasn't mine became a survival strategy.

But life also has a way of deepening our compassion through shared struggle. The experiences that shaped me most haven't only been my own, they've been the ones I've walked through beside someone I love.

And nothing revealed that truth more clearly than the day I almost lost my son.

— -

A Memory That Never Left Me

I knew his pain.
 I had felt it before.
 And I had witnessed it in someone I loved.

Jenny and I had been friends since elementary school. Girl Scouts, shared friend groups, years of laughter and growing up side by side. She was bubbly and silly, sassy and bright. Beautiful, with a laugh that could stretch on for hours. She worked hard and played hard, and to most people, she looked like she was doing just fine.

But I saw what most others didn't.

Somewhere along the way, we bonded not just through friendship, but through shared pain. We both smiled easily on the outside while quietly carrying things that felt too heavy for girls our age. There was a sadness in her: a darkness she didn't often detail but it lived beneath the surface. Sometimes we confessed feeling misunderstood, empty and lost. But mostly, we tried to forget. It was a relief to be with someone who understood without explanation.

After graduation, I moved away. Life pulled us in different directions, and we lost touch; as young adults often do, assuming there will always be time to reconnect.

Then came the call.

Jenny was twenty-four when she took her life—one fatal gunshot. At that age, death still felt abstract. We weren't thinking about endings. We were just beginning our stories. The shock rippled through all of us who loved her, leaving behind grief layered with questions that never fully settle.

I've replayed it countless times since.
  What if I had reached out more?
  What if I had asked harder questions?
  Would it have made a difference for her, or for me?

During the loneliest moments of my first marriage, I used to visit her grave. When the weight of conflict, disappointment, and his drinking felt unbearable, I'd sit there and talk to her. I cried. I prayed. I asked God for strength. For clarity. For relief.

Standing there, I could feel how heavy her world must have felt—how final it all became. And I recognized something familiar in myself. I understood how despair can shrink your vision until hope feels barely visible.

But I also understood this: I never wanted to reach that point.

Visiting her grave became a reminder: not that life is fragile, but that it is still worth holding onto. That even the smallest glimmer of hope matters. That nothing is so hard it cannot be weathered through.

In fifth grade, we'd drawn names for a secret Santa exchange in Girl Scouts. Jenny had my name. She gave me a small gold-plated ornament, etched by hand:

"Friends Forever. Love, Jenny."

To this day, it hangs near the top of my Christmas tree. My quiet holiday angel. Every year, I wonder who she might have been by now. How many children. Maybe grandchildren. The relationships we would have laughed about. The stories we never got to share.

And when my son stood on the edge of his own darkness years later, all I could think was:

I did not want this ending for him.

I wanted, desperately, to carry him out of the shadows.

—-

A Mother's Plea

My oldest son called me early one morning. Heartbroken, anxious, and spiraling. I talked him through a severe panic attack, then encouraged him to get outside, breathe the fresh air, nourish his body, and promised to check in later. I could feel his fragility before he even said a word.

That evening, he didn't answer my text. Or my call. Or the next one.

Panic rose as every attempt went straight to voicemail. I left a message no mother ever wants to leave, telling him to call me back or I'd show up at his door or contact the police for a wellness check.

When he finally returned my call, I knew immediately that something was very wrong.

He was emotional, overwhelmed, intoxicated, and speaking from a place of deep despair. Then, with a trembling honesty, he quietly admitted that earlier that day—holding a loaded gun—he had been moments away from ending his life. He felt numb. Exhausted. Lost.

My body shook and tears streamed down my face as I listened. He was driving. I didn't know where. The gun was in the car. I pleaded with God for the right words. I begged my son to hold on to hope, to breathe. To pull over. To remember the people who loved him. To give his pain and his struggle to God.

His voice cracked as he whispered, "Mom, I have been. I'm tired. It doesn't seem to do any good."

What terrified me most wasn't only what he had almost done, it was how disconnected he sounded from himself, his faith, and the world around him.

After what seemed like forever, he eventually agreed to stop driving, put the weapon away, and rest. Only when I knew he was home did my body finally collapse in relief.

The days that followed were filled with emotion, gratitude, and sobering clarity. My son began to return to himself. Standing next to him at church that following Sunday, worship rising around us, I wept in thanksgiving. For protection. For second chances. For breath. For the reminder that life can shift in an instant: that love is often the thin thread that keeps us tethered here.

Even now, I replay that night. How heartbreak, substance use, and depression can collide into something unbearable. How fragile life is. How deeply we need one another.

I had seen where despair can lead and I knew how fiercely I wanted him to stay.

— -

We Need Each Other

No matter what we face—grief, loss, fear, joy, or triumph—life is not meant to be lived alone.

We are here to hold space for one another. To sit in the dark with someone until the light returns. To remind each other that hope is still possible.

If you think you are alone, you aren't.
　　If you think nobody will understand, someone will.

If you think your pain is too heavy, someone can help you carry it.

We were designed for connection: for shared burdens, shared healing, shared humanity.

PERSONAL INSIGHT

This experience taught me that loving someone doesn't always mean rescuing them or carrying their pain for them. It means remaining present while they navigate their own storm. I learned long ago what it feels like to lose someone to despair, and I learned again what it means to nearly lose someone I love. Both shaped me.

Sometimes God doesn't remove the pain. Instead, He sends us to sit beside one another in it; steady, loving, and unwilling to let go. Shared suffering doesn't weaken us; it deepens compassion and expands our capacity to love in ways we never expected.

TAKEAWAY

Healing often happens through relationship, not isolation. Compassion grows when we allow ourselves to see and feel one another's pain. You don't need the perfect words. You only need presence, patience, and faith that God is working in ways you cannot see.

SOUL NUGGETS

- *You don't have to fix the storm, just stay with someone in it.*
- *Compassion is born where hearts break open.*
- *We survive by leaning on each other.*
- *Presence is often the miracle.*

REFLECTION / JOURNAL PROMPTS

1. When have you carried someone else's pain? What did it teach you about love?

2. Who has walked beside you during a season when you felt fragile or afraid?

3. Where might God be inviting you to show up for someone; not to fix them, but to be present with them?

4. What does "shared suffering" mean to you, and how has it shaped your relationships?

If this chapter stirred something tender or difficult, additional support resources are available at the back of this book. You don't have to navigate this alone.

WHEN LIFE REOPENS AN OLD WOUND, IT'S NOT A SETBACK, IT'S AN *invitation* TO HEAL DEEPER.

#AThousandSmallResurrections

17

Healing Isn't Linear

Often, the days start to blur together: kids' activities, work, chores, maybe a holiday or quick getaway thrown in the mix. The ups and downs of everyday life keep you in motion. No matter the circumstances, you somehow find your rhythm. You blink, and years are gone. If not for social media memories or the photos on your phone, you might not even recall when things happened.

But then there are those moments that freeze in time—
the ones where you remember exactly where you were,
what song was playing,
what you were wearing,
and who you were with.

That day in June, when I got the message from my sister, was one of those moments.

It was a short text:
"Can you meet? I need to talk."

Mind you, this is not how my sister communicates. She rarely texts—and certainly not like that. We usually video chat. I knew something was wrong, so I didn't ask questions. We quickly decided to meet at our usual lunch spot—halfway between our homes, about a twenty-minute drive each.

My sister—my ride or die, my other half—has been the only one who's walked beside me through everything. Two years apart in age, we've shared clothes, toys, rooms, friends (maybe even a boy crush or two), holidays, vacations, parenting schedules, and family dramas/traumas. The inside jokes and dark secrets no one else could ever understand? She does.

People often mistake us for twins. We both have a creative streak and even attended the same college, earning the same degree. Our lives have mirrored each other in many ways—both divorced twice, both raising four kids. For me, one girl and three boys. For her, one boy and three girls.

And yet, we couldn't be more different.

She's the funny, adventurous, spontaneous one. I'm the thoughtful, organized, emotional one.

Ask either of us about our childhood and we could finish each other's sentences. Like how we both fell apart during our dad's "interrogations," him being the retired police officer. What it was like to split every holiday between four different families. How we'd joke about mom's meatloaf, the wooden spoon she used as punishment, or call her, "Mommy Dearest" just to see her reaction. We may remember things slightly different, but no one understands me like she does.

That afternoon at the restaurant, she didn't waste a moment. She began to share what had unfolded the day before—and then came the part she could barely speak.

"He placed a hidden camera in the bathroom to video her in the shower."

Time stopped.

She sat across from me, staring blankly, her eyes saying everything her lips couldn't. Tears tried to hide the darkness behind them—the portal to a heart that had been completely shattered, the light sucked right out.

I sat there in shock, hands over my mouth in horror.

Her husband.
  Her partner.
  The soulmate she thought was forever.

Caught trying to film his stepdaughter in the shower.

We didn't have to speak; our minds were racing in sync.

My niece.
  Her daughter.
  My sister.
  Her marriage.
  Their family.
  Our past.

It felt like a nightmare in broad daylight. This was the one thing—*the one thing*—we had always feared most. Something like this happening to our kids. She even said, through tears, "Of all the things... I could've handled cheating, but this?"

And then my niece.

Oh, my sweet niece.

In that moment, I felt her pain as if it were my own. Her confusion. Her trauma. She had found the camera. She knew what it was.

A wave of memories flooded me: my own childhood, my own bathroom scenes, my stepdad's betrayal. My heart broke for her, knowing how those feelings could echo for a lifetime. I wanted to run to her, hold her, and take it all away.

The days, weeks, and months that followed were heavy. We all did our best to navigate the shock, the grief, and the steps that came next.

But the beginning was not gentle. My niece wasn't just traumatized; she was angry, hurt, and deeply conflicted by what happened. By her mom's initial responses. By the confusion and fractured sense of safety that often follow something like this. There was resentment there too— the kind that comes when the person you need most feels momentarily unavailable or unsure how to protect you.

That rupture—the pain of not feeling immediately seen or defended— was painfully familiar to me. I had once carried that same mix of love and resentment toward a parent I still needed. Because I understood that wound from the inside, I found myself trying to soften edges and hold space for emotions that had nowhere else to land.

—-

Just when you think you've done all the healing work: the therapy, the journaling, the meditating; life throws a curveball that cracks you open again, exposing wounds that still need tending.

This wasn't my story. But it ran painfully parallel to mine.

I wasn't just witnessing her anger; I was remembering my own.

I didn't want my triggers to overshadow what they were going through. So, I went back to therapy to process my own resurfaced pain privately, to keep their healing separate from mine. I needed to be grounded for them, to see through their lens, not my own.

—-

I am so proud of my niece. I watched in awe as she bravely secured the evidence and spoke up by reporting to the authorities, filing a report, and writing a letter that was powerfully read aloud by the judge at the hearing. She asked for maximum charges allowed without a trial. It wasn't easy, but her courage to stand up for herself... that was everything.

Something I've spent years wishing I had done for myself.

And I am also proud of my sister for facing the collapse of the life she thought she knew, and for choosing and protecting her daughter. It was a rough road at first, but she found her footing: getting sober, confronting her own childhood trauma, and rebuilding her life as a single mom. With her newfound strength, she stood beside her daughter, listened, encouraged, and supported her. She turned her pain into purpose, too.

PERSONAL INSIGHT

Healing isn't just about our own pain. Sometimes it's about standing beside someone else in theirs; holding steady, even when it stirs our own buried wounds. This moment with my sister and niece reminded me that healing isn't a straight path: it's more like a spiral.

We circle back to old places, not because we've failed, but because we're ready to meet them with new eyes: wiser, softer, stronger. Each return is its own small resurrection. Something old rises, but so does something new.

TAKEAWAYS

Healing isn't a finish line we cross. It's a journey that continually reshapes us.

When someone we love is hurting, our own wounds often rise to the surface. Not to weaken us, but to awaken us. These echoes aren't evidence of slipping backward; they're reminders of the tenderness still inside us.

Real healing happens when we allow ourselves to be present for others without losing ourselves, when we honor what rises in us without letting it overshadow their pain.

Sometimes the most sacred work we can do is tend to our own heart quietly, so we can show up with strength, clarity, and love.

SOUL NUGGETS

- *Returning to old wounds doesn't mean you failed. It means you survived long enough to heal them again.*
- *Your triggers are teachers, not punishments.*
- *What breaks you open can also raise you higher toward truth, compassion, and purpose.*
- *You can hold someone else's pain without abandoning your own.*

REFLECTION / JOURNAL PROMPTS

1. When was the last time someone else's pain stirred up something tender in you? What did it reveal?

2. What part of your past still echoes in moments of vulnerability or crisis?

3. How do you recognize when you're carrying someone else's burden

instead of simply supporting them?

4. Where in your healing journey have you noticed the spiral; returning to similar emotions with more clarity or strength?

5. What does it look like for you to show up for others without losing yourself in their story?

** If this story struck something in you, resources for support and healing are available at the back of this book. Help is one of the ways God meets us in our need.*

MY VOICE IS *sacred.*

MY BOUNDARIES ARE *holy.*

MY STORY IS *mine to tell.*

#AThousandSmallResurrections

18

Not Your Free Pass

When I look back now, I can see it clearly. But at the time, I didn't know I was being shaped.

Some stories don't begin with words. They begin in the body.
In the tightening of your chest.
In the instinct to freeze.
In the quiet calculation of how to make it through without making it worse.

For a long time, I didn't name what was happening to me—not because I couldn't, but because I didn't know I was allowed to. It felt ordinary. Expected. Common. The kind of thing you were supposed to brush off, laugh about, tolerate.

The comments were dismissed as harmless.
The looks excused.
The hands minimized.

I told myself it didn't matter. That this was simply part of being a woman. That speaking up wouldn't change anything because it happened everywhere, to everyone.

But silence is not neutral. It reshapes you.

It settles into your body and becomes posture, breath, instinct. You learn when to smile, when to stay small, when to adjust yourself to make others more comfortable. You learn to question yourself instead of the behavior.

Over time, those moments become mirrors—reflecting distorted messages about your worth, your boundaries, your right to take up space.

Long before I had language for power or consent, my body understood.

And it remembered.

—-

The Pattern

This wasn't an isolated experience. This was a pattern that took shape early and repeated itself in different forms, different faces, different places.

My stepdad, as I've mentioned. But there were more.

Boys in the school hallways—grabbing, whispering, crossing lines they had no right to cross. At football games, house parties, a friend's basement: there was always someone testing boundaries. Someone who thought my body was public property.

A grab at my breasts.

A hand between my legs or from behind.
Someone trying to lift my skirt "just to see if they could."

I remember freezing. Laughing nervously. Pretending it didn't matter.

But it did.

As an adult, it's been the eyes that linger too long. Comments about my looks, my walk, my body. On a dance floor, at a bar, in a crowded room—a stranger's hand that finds its way to my body as if the space between us belongs to them.

The dates: those who assume dinner and conversation come with an unspoken expectation. That my kindness is a promise. That a "no" means "convince me."

Dating apps that have some sending vulgar messages or requesting personal photos before even knowing your full name.

And, the workplace: the space I hoped would be professional, safe, respectful.

Even there, I've learned over time to navigate the same tightrope: avoiding certain offices, enduring "friendly" hugs, smiling politely at sexist jokes. Some conversations aren't about work at all, but about power.

There have been higher-ups who manipulated situations to blur the lines—a business trip, a work conference, an empty office, a closed door. The subtle shift from mentor to predator.

Once, a colleague invited me to dinner and drinks to discuss a potential partnership. I showed up excited, ambitious, prepared to talk business.

But as the evening progressed, he made it clear the opportunity was conditional—sexual access in exchange for professional advancement.

The air left the room.

It wasn't just humiliation; It was déjà vu.
    The same story, different setting.

Sexual abuse.
    Sexual assault.
    Sexual harassment.

I've experienced them all.

— -

The Beliefs I Carried

Early on, I learned through experience that how I looked determined how I was treated.
    That attention equaled worthiness.
    That beauty meant value.
    That I was loved as long as I was pretty.

If I could control how others saw me, maybe I could control what happened to me.

But I couldn't.

What once looked like empowerment was really survival. Gaining attention didn't fill me; it emptied me. I felt vulnerable, unseen, misunderstood.

I also realized that being kind, genuine, or empathetic was often misinterpreted. People assumed I was flirting when I was just being friendly. My warmth was mistaken for invitation. My smile, for consent.

But my smile is **not** your free pass to my body.
My kindness is **not** permission.
My empathy is **not** an open door for disrespect.

—-

The Turning Point

For years, I carried those experiences quietly. They lived inside me, accumulating in ways I didn't even realize. The shame. The confusion. The guilt for things that weren't mine to carry.

Then, one day, I stopped pretending it didn't matter.

Having watched my niece navigate her story—empowered and un-apologetic in taking a stance for herself—I felt something shift in me: I was worth fighting for too.

When a workplace situation crossed the line and a man in power took advantage of me, I finally spoke up. At first to him. Then formally, hiring an attorney.

I filed the report. I answered the questions. I walked through every uncomfortable step that followed.

It wasn't about money. It wasn't about punishment.
    It was about reclaiming my power.

Standing up for myself in that moment felt like reclaiming every younger version of me who froze, who laughed it off, who swallowed the pain and humiliation.

For the first time, I didn't minimize what happened.
    I didn't excuse it.
    And I didn't carry it alone.

The victory wasn't legal—it was spiritual. It was the quiet reclaiming of my dignity, my voice, my worth.

— -

The Healing

It's taken years to untangle the warped beliefs those experiences formed inside me. To understand deeply that:

None of it was my fault.
    I didn't "invite" it.
    I didn't cause it.
    I didn't deserve it.

My looks, my kindness, my presence; those things were never the problem. They are gifts. They are parts of me that deserve to exist safely.

I've learned healing isn't about erasing what happened. It's about releasing what was never mine to carry. It's about learning to love myself in all the places the world tried to wound.

Today, I walk differently.

I hold my head higher. I still lead with kindness, but I no longer confuse kindness with compliance.

I take up space without apology.

True strength doesn't have to be loud or forceful.

Sometimes it's the soft whisper of "no more."

Sometimes it's filing the report.

Sometimes it's walking away.

And sometimes it's just looking in the mirror and saying:

You didn't deserve that.

But you survived it.

And you are free now.

I've got you.

This is what resurrection looks like sometimes: not loud, not dramatic; just choosing rest, boundaries, truth, and the courage to rise as who you really are.

PERSONAL INSIGHT

Every time I speak my truth, I loosen the grip of shame that never belonged to me.

Every time I name what happened, I reclaim a part of my soul that was once silenced.

And every time I choose healing over hiding, I remind myself:

I am whole.

I am worthy.

I am free.

This was the moment I rose. Not dramatically, not loudly; just firmly, finally.

Our stories are not stains. They are sacred maps of survival.

They show us where we've been and reveal the grace that carried us forward.

Pain may have been part of your story, but it is not your identity.

You are not what was done to you.

You are what you chose to rise from.

TAKEAWAYS

Boundaries are sacred. You are allowed to protect your body, your time, your energy, and your peace.

Your voice is your power. Speaking up is not about revenge, it is about liberation.

You owe no one access to you. Your body is not community property.

Kindness is not consent. Warmth is not invitation.

Healing begins when you stop blaming yourself. The shame belongs to the one who crossed the line, not the one who endured it.

SOUL NUGGETS

- *You are not responsible for the comfort of those who crossed your lines.*
- *You can be soft and strong at the same time. Both are holy.*
- *Your freedom is not up for negotiation.*
- *You are worthy of safety, respect, and honor in every room you walk into.*

REFLECTION / JOURNAL PROMPTS

1. What moments in your life taught you to stay silent? What might freedom sound like now?

2. Where have you confused kindness with obligation? How can you honor your empathy without abandoning your boundaries?

3. In what ways can you begin to view your experiences not as shameful, but as proof of your resilience and strength?

4. Write a letter to your younger self; the one who froze, who laughed it off, who didn't know how to say no. Tell her what you know now.

154

155

** For readers seeking support—for themselves or someone they love—a list of trusted resources can be found at the back of this book.*

MONEY REVEALS WHERE WE FEAR LACK, BUT *trust* REMINDS US WE ARE *provided for.*

#AThousandSmallResurrections

19

The Wealth of Surrender

The Currency of Survival

My relationship with money has always been complicated. It is one of the most triggering, emotionally charged areas of my life. Just thinking about it can create the same physical response I feel when one of my trauma triggers gets activated. My stomach twists. My chest tightens. Sleep becomes elusive. Money has always carried a hum of anxiety for me. I grew up believing there would never be enough.

When I was younger, part of why I never spoke out about my abuse was because I didn't think we could afford to leave. My parents worried constantly about money. Bills were a regular source of stress, and sometimes even groceries felt uncertain. I learned early that financial stability—or the lack of it—determined whether we stayed or went, whether we felt safe or scared.

As I grew up, I carried those same fears with me.

After betrayal in my first marriage, survival shaped every decision. I was pregnant, unemployed, living far from home, and had no money. Under those circumstances, staying didn't feel like a choice. It felt like the only option I had.

We were a young military family trying to make ends meet. We had very little and often relied on government assistance to get by. Every paycheck felt like a lifeline. As time went on, we worked hard to build some sense of stability but debt often buried us. Eventually, we filed bankruptcy. At the time, it felt like failure—a painful reminder of how fragile stability really was.

We recovered and rebuilt. But not long after finding financial footing, our marriage collapsed. Again, the foundation I thought I could depend on—emotionally and financially—crumbled beneath me.

Then came life on my own as a single mom of two. I worked 50-plus hours a week just to keep a roof over our heads and food on the table. I was determined to stay afloat, to protect my credit, to give my kids some sense of stability. I managed, but it wasn't easy.

My anxiety around money never really went away; it just changed shape. Sometimes it showed up as procrastination. I would avoid opening bills or checking my bank account, even when I had enough to cover things. Money made me feel exposed, tense, and afraid of failing. The fear lived just beneath the surface.

When I remarried, my husband handled our finances. For the first time, I felt relief. Like maybe I could finally exhale. The burden of managing our money wouldn't rest solely on my shoulders. When he suggested I default on my mortgage to reduce debt so we could move into our future home, I was hesitant. I had worked so hard for that place. But he assured me he'd take care of us and encouraged me to release my grip on the past. I trusted him. I walked away from my mortgage, ruining my credit, and handed over the responsibility of managing our money.

But eventually, I realized I'd surrendered more than the task—I'd surrendered my power. The part of me that wanted to feel cared for had unintentionally silenced the part of me that needed to stay engaged and aware.

And then the familiar pattern resurfaced. I found myself betrayed again—pregnant, unemployed, my credit destroyed—and unable to see a viable path to leaving. It was the exact same trap as before, just wrapped in a different life.

As tension escalated in our marriage over the years, the idea of leaving felt impossible because of our financial situation. I later discovered major financial decisions had been made without my knowledge or consent, involving our savings and home equity, and not turning out as hoped. I was shocked and devastated. **Betrayal is betrayal**, whether it's emotional, physical, or financial. And having survived heart surgery only a year earlier, a reminder of how life can change in an instant, this hit even harder. Our future seemed uncertain, our security thin.

When he decided we could no longer afford to stay in our home, I saw an opening, a way back to myself. I suggested a separation. It became both an ending and a beginning. A moment of reclaiming what had been lost, not just spiritually but financially too.

Money was still tight, but I gave myself grace. Every step forward, every decision made with clarity instead of fear, every bill paid with peace instead of panic became a small act of healing. I didn't know it then, but this was resurrection in its simplest form—rising inch by inch into a life I had once believed was possible for me.

Shortly after moving out on my own, life tested me again. Due to circumstances beyond my control, I had to walk away from my job and went nearly nine months without work. I sent out hundreds of resumes. Nothing came through in the marketing and design field I'd spent twenty-five years in. I watched my savings slowly drain. Unemployment ran out. Eventually, I needed government assistance again. Fear crept in; whispering that I was about to lose everything I had rebuilt.

But something in me shifted this time. I surrendered. I prayed for God to help me heal my anxious relationship with money. I asked to see finances as a flow of energy: coming and going freely and effortlessly, instead of something I needed to white-knuckle.

Almost immediately, I felt an unexplainable peace.

I still showed up each day, applying for jobs, staying open; but I no longer carried the weight alone. Then just when I needed it most, resources, support, and unexpected connections began to appear. My body relaxed. The tension, anxious energy, and racing thoughts no longer had its grip on me. Instead, my focus became researching financial education courses and resources. Knowledge felt like power.

Soon after, I was presented with an opportunity to interview for a position I had very little experience in: finance. To my surprise, I was hired into a finance-related role, working with numbers and systems I once felt intimidated by—something I never imagined I would be doing. It was exciting to grow and learn in an area I felt so small and weak. This new opportunity made me feel empowered and strong. It felt like being guided not just out of lack, but into a new identity, one born from everything I had endured.

Not only did God provide for me exactly when my situation felt bleak, but He guided me into a role that would strengthen the very area I had always felt most powerless.

I realized something profound: **peace doesn't come from having enough; it comes from trusting that you will be provided for.**

I'm grateful to have reclaimed my power.

My relationship with money, and with myself, is still evolving. But now it's rooted in trust, grace, and a quiet knowing that I am never truly without what I need.

I also believe that power comes when you face your struggles head on instead of running from or burying them. Fear teaches us to hide, retreat and stay small. But the moment we can name our insecurities and ask ourselves what small steps can we take to grow, learn and act on, we begin to change the narrative our past traumas wrote for us.

This is the wealth of surrender: the moment you stop clinging to the life that broke you and rise into the one that is finally ready to hold you.

PERSONAL INSIGHT

Money is never just about money. It carries our stories; our fears, our upbringing, our relationships, our survival. For most of my life, finances represented danger, instability, and dependency. But life continuously invited me to rewrite that story.

What I learned is that healing in this area doesn't start with numbers on a page. It starts with reclaiming your story, trusting yourself again, and opening to the possibility that you are supported in more ways than you can see.

TAKEAWAYS

Your relationship with money reflects your relationship with safety, self-worth, and trust. When you begin approaching your finances with awareness instead of avoidance, compassion instead of shame, and trust instead of fear, you begin rewriting generations of scarcity.

Every calm choice you make—whether opening a bill, asking a question, or learning something new—becomes an act of healing.

Surrender opens doors effort cannot. When you release what you cannot carry, God moves in ways you never could have orchestrated on your own.

SOUL NUGGETS

- *Money reveals where we fear lack, but trust reminds us we are provided for.*

- *Financial trauma is real and healing is possible.*
- *Reclaiming your financial power is reclaiming your future.*

REFLECTION / JOURNAL PROMPTS

1. What early memories shaped the way you view money, safety, and security?

2. When you think about money, what sensations arise in your body and what past experiences do they connect to?

3. Where have you given away your financial power (through fear, avoidance, or blind trust)?

4. What small, grounded steps can you take to approach money with curiosity, gratitude, or stewardship rather than anxiety?

5. How do you define "enough" right now and how might God be inviting you to redefine it?

worth

IS NOT

MEASURED

BY WHAT WE

GIVE, DO, OR

PRODUCE.

#AThousandSmallResurrections

20

The Heaviness of Carrying It All

I've always been the one people could count on.

The one who said yes. The one who helped, fixed, created, organized, and made things beautiful. I could plan the perfect party, design the perfect website, paint the perfect wall, or solve the problem no one else could seem to.

On the outside, it looked like generosity—and in many ways, it was. I love creating. I love helping. I love seeing someone's face light up when something I've done makes their life a little easier or a little more beautiful.

But underneath that drive was something else—a need to prove, to please, to earn love through effort.

I didn't know it at the time, but I was using *doing* as a way to feel safe.

—-

When Doing Becomes a Disguise for Worth

Looking back, I can see it now—how much I gave without ever asking for much in return.

I would spend hours creating custom designs, hosting events, decorating spaces, or offering my skills, often for free or far below what I deserved.

I told myself I was just being kind. That it was "good exposure," or that I didn't mind because I loved it.

But beneath those reasons was a quieter truth:
"Your comfort matters more than mine."
"Your needs are worth more than my worth."

Each time I undercharged or overgave, I was silently agreeing with the lie that my time—and by extension, I—wasn't enough.

Eventually, the things that once filled me began to drain me.
What used to spark joy became another obligation.
The things I loved most became the very things that left me depleted.

— -

The Pattern Beneath the Pattern

Perfectionism. Overcommitting. Overextending. Fixing.
They all wear different faces, but they share the same heartbeat.

Control as safety.

When you grow up in chaos, pain, or unpredictability, your nervous system learns to survive by doing.

If you can't control what others do, you learn to control yourself: your performance, your output, your usefulness.

So I became the helper, the doer, the strong one.

I kept peace, even at the expense of my own.

I believed that love had to be earned, not simply received.

I thought my worth was tied to what I could give, how perfect I could make things, or how well I could anticipate a need before it was spoken.

But all that giving came at a cost—my rest, my creativity, my joy, my self-worth.

—-

When "Enough" Finally Speaks

The more I've healed, the more I've realized that I can't do it anymore.

Not because I've stopped caring but because my spirit is tired of running on empty.

Tired of trying to earn something that was mine all along.

I've started to see that my need to fix, give, or perform isn't always coming from love—sometimes it's from fear.

Fear of letting someone down.

Fear of being unneeded.

Fear of being invisible or undervalued.

Fear of being considered selfish if I said no, or "not enough" if I didn't say yes.

But love without boundaries isn't love. It's depletion dressed up as devotion.

—-

The Healing: Learning to Receive

Healing means slowing down. It means saying "no" without apology and "yes" with intention.

It means charging what I'm worth. Not because money defines me, but because energy has value, and what I create comes from my soul.

I am beginning to see that giving and receiving are not opposites; they're a sacred balance.

To pour into others, I have to first be filled.

To truly serve, I have to start from wholeness, not from fear.

And God reminded me:

"Come to me, all you who are weary and carry heavy burdens, and I will give you rest." — Matthew 11:28 (NLT)

I was never meant to hold it all.

Not every burden is mine to carry.

Not every problem is mine to fix.

Not every need is mine to meet.

I am allowed to be at peace.
  I am allowed to rest.
  I am allowed to receive.

PERSONAL INSIGHT

I used to think that the more I did, the more worthy I would become.
  But now I know the truth: I was enough before I ever lifted a finger.

Safety isn't found in control; it's found in trust.
  Peace doesn't come from doing. It comes from being.
  Love isn't earned. It's received.
  And I no longer have to prove anything to be held, seen, or valued.

TAKEAWAYS

Your worth is inherent, not earned. Who you are matters more than what you do.

Overgiving is often a sign of old wounds, not present-day obligations. It reveals the beliefs built in survival, not the truth of who you are now.

Boundaries are a form of self-respect, not rejection. Saying no is not rejection; it's honoring your soul. It's how you protect your energy, your peace, and your capacity.

Your most powerful giving comes from overflow, not depletion. You were never meant to pour from emptiness.

SOUL NUGGETS

- *Rest and boundaries are not selfish, they are sacred.*
- *Saying no to what drains you makes room for what fulfills you.*
- *You no longer have to prove your value. You can simply live it.*
- *You are allowed to be held, supported, and filled too.*

REFLECTION / JOURNAL PROMPTS

1. Where in your life do you find yourself saying "yes" when your soul is whispering "no"?

2. What part of you still believes love or approval must be earned?

3. How do you feel when others offer to help you? What comes up? Resistance? Guilt? Relief?

4. What would it look like to honor your time, gifts, and energy the same way you honor others'?

5. If you stopped doing so much, what fear rises first? And what truth rises right behind it?

FROM OUR

FIRST

breath

TO OUR LAST, WE

ARE WIRED FOR

connection.

#AThousandSmallResurrections

21

Born in Connection, Returned in Love

Life has a way of reminding us that none of us were meant to walk this world alone.

I've been blessed to carry three of my own children to term and to experience each one enter the world. I've also witnessed my niece and nephew being born, along with two of my granddaughters. No matter how many times I've been in that space, nothing prepares you for the miracle of a first breath.

Birth is a holy unveiling.

The quiet strength of a mother's body, the courage of a child entering the unknown, the deep inhale of life beginning—every moment feels sacred.

Those first moments of skin-to-skin contact hold a magic all their own. The way a baby instinctively settles at the sound of the mother's voice. The way their tiny bodies find warmth, safety, and regulation just by resting against a beating heart.

Research tells us what our souls already know: skin-to-skin contact stabilizes a newborn's temperature, heart rate, breathing, and stress hormones. It increases breastfeeding, reduces postpartum depression and anxiety, and strengthens the parent–child bond.

From the first breath we take, we need connection.
  It is our lifeline.
  It is our beginning.

—-

I've also held space for loved ones as they've taken their last breath— as their soul slipped from its earthly body and returned home. It is heartbreaking, it is tender, and profoundly beautiful.

Not everyone experiences birth or death in the same way. But what I know is this: both are sacred thresholds. Both are divine miracles. And both become even more meaningful when we move through them together.

In the end, we are all souls having a human experience—longing to feel seen, understood, and held.

—-

My grandma Jo was woven into the fabric of my daily life. She moved in with us when I was in elementary school and stayed well after I graduated. The youngest of ten, standing just four-foot-eleven with striking jet-black hair and cheekbones that reflected her Indian heritage proudly—she was unforgettable.

Grandma Jo was a spitfire with a dry sense of humor. She often kept to herself so she wouldn't be a burden, but yet it wasn't uncommon to find her either at the kitchen table, playing bingo, watching baseball, doing crosswords, or enjoying old movies.

When we moved back from North Carolina in my late twenties, she helped watch my kids as I returned to work. Those years were a gift for all of us.

As she grew older, I cherished every visit. I loved hearing her stories, pieces of a life lived long before mine began. It's funny how, as children, we rarely imagine our parents or grandparents having full lives before us, childhoods, dreams, heartbreaks, adventures. But when they speak of them, their souls come alive.

As her memory began to fade from Dementia, we had her write down some of her stories. I'm grateful we captured them, snapshots of love, wisdom and resilience.

When her final day came, my mom, sister, and I gathered around her bedside. Three generations of women. We shared memories, combed her hair, massaged her hands and feet, played songs she loved, and quoted her favorite movie. We laughed. We cried. We told her she had been our home.

We told her it was okay to go. That her family was waiting.

While my mom and sister stepped outside, I stayed with her. I held her hand and prayed over her. I asked God to bring her peacefully into His kingdom.

And just like that—she slipped away.

The stillness wasn't dark; it was light.
  Sacred.
  Holy.
  A blessing.

— -

Just shy of a year later, my daughter gave birth to my youngest granddaughter. Her middle name: Jo.

She arrived with the same dark hair and complexion as her great-great-grandmother. The connection was undeniable.

Holding her for the first time, I felt the fullness of the circle of life. How we come into this world to experience humanness—to learn, to grow, to shape and be shaped by the ones walking alongside us. We are here to be gifts to one another.

To show up.
  To love.
  To raise the vibration of the collective.

It's no surprise baby Jo looks identical to photos of grandma Jo at the same age. Even as a toddler, she gravitated toward pictures of a woman she never met. It was as though she knew her somehow. Now at four, her mannerisms remind us of her often. Sweet and spunky, gentle and bold. A new generation, yet a bridge to generations past.

And so it continues, life folding into death, death making space for life, each breath connected to the ones who came before us and the ones who will come after.

Birth giving way to loss, loss making room for new life, and love threading them all together.

PERSONAL INSIGHT

What I've come to learn is that life and death are not opposites: they are sacred companions in the human experience. One ushers us in. One carries us home. Both remind us that connection is essential.

I've been blessed through personal experience to realize that we are meant to walk one another in, walk one another home, and walk beside each other in every season in between.

TAKEAWAYS

Your life touches countless lives: far more than what you can see. The way you love, show up, remember, honor, and stand beside others becomes part of the legacy you leave.

Life is not meant to be carried alone. It is meant to be shared, witnessed, and held in community.

Every beginning echoes an ending. Every ending makes room for a new beginning. That is the quiet resurrection woven into the human story.

SOUL NUGGETS

- *Birth and death are sacred mirrors; they remind us what truly matters.*
- *Your presence is a blessing in someone's story.*
- *Love is a thread that outlives every ending.*
- *Every generation is a resurrection of the ones who came before.*

REFLECTION / JOURNAL PROMPTS

1. Who has walked with you through sacred thresholds: births, losses, transitions? How did it change you?

2. What parts of your own family lineage do you carry forward? What wisdom or traits feel like gifts passed down?

3. How do you want to show up for others in their beginnings, endings, or in-between seasons?

4. What does "being a blessing" mean to you in your current season of life?

5. If you were to write a letter to a future generation, what essence of your life would you want them to remember?

LOVE CAN BUILD
A HOME, BUT
EVERY *heart*
STILL HAS ITS OWN
JOURNEY TOWARD
belonging.

#AThousandSmallResurrections

22

The Many Rooms of Belonging

Adoption isn't my story—at least not in the sense that I was adopted. But it has shaped the landscape of my life in ways that have marked me more deeply than I realized for many years.

I grew up knowing I had an older brother somewhere out in the world. My mom had been open with my sister and me about it, as it had always been hard for her to live knowing she had a son she couldn't connect with. He had been born when my parents were just teenagers—kids themselves—and the decision to place him for adoption wasn't even theirs. It was made by my grandparents, and the judge. The adults in the room.

When my brother went in search of his birth family at eighteen, and reunited with us, our world shifted. I still remember the day he arrived—this stranger who looked like us, carried pieces of our features, our talents, our dad's mannerisms, and yet carried a whole life before us. It was strange but exciting to finally meet him. I had always wondered what he would be like.

Our mom was elated. And at first, my dad and stepmom welcomed him too, including him in a few family gatherings and even a trip to the Boundary Waters; a long weekend camping adventure with just my sister, my brother, and our dad. And then, almost without warning, they shut the door. They decided they wanted no relationship with him at all.

This put my sister and me right in the middle. Like a tug-of-war we never asked to play. My dad and stepmom acted as if he didn't exist, ignoring him or offering only casual "hello's" when they picked my sister and me up for our weekend visits.

Watching the rejection unfold did something inside me. As a girl already living with the secret trauma of my stepdad's abuse, it planted a deeper fear: *What would it take for them to disown me too?* I even asked that question once. Their answer didn't make sense to me. The question stayed.

And our brother—already carrying the weight of being given up once—resented for years that my sister and I didn't stand up for him after our dad's rejection. In his eyes, we didn't defend him. In our hearts, we were terrified to rock the boat. We didn't want to be next. The fear of losing my relationship with them kept me silent, even when silence hurt someone I loved.

Meanwhile, our mom poured most of her time and energy into trying to reclaim the years she lost with her son. It was hard to watch him come in and receive from my mom the kind of attention I had been starving for.

I loved that he was there. But there was a quiet ache in me, a hurt girl wondering why she hadn't been enough to fight for, while someone else could just show up and be chosen.

My sister and I were stretched between two families, two loyalties, two worlds. There was no safe side to stand on.

— -

And then there were my adopted siblings, my younger brother and sister, two beautiful souls from Korea whom my dad and stepmom brought into our family when I was in my early teens.

With every new arrival, I questioned my place a little more. Not because I didn't love them, I did, fiercely, but because the ground underneath me felt unstable.

My younger siblings may have wrestled with belonging, their own questions of identity and connection. And I, the non-adopted child, found myself wrestling with my own version of displacement.

— -

And then, marriage offered me another lesson in chosen family—this time through *my* role as a stepmom.

Becoming a stepmom reshaped my understanding of belonging. My stepson lived with us full-time, and loving him opened a different wing of my heart. A room I didn't know existed until I stepped into it. I adored him, but step parenting isn't simple. It comes with invisible layers: loyalty binds, fears you don't name, and the quiet hope that your love is landing in the places they need it most.

There were days I felt unsure or unsteady, wondering if I was enough for him... or if I was overstepping in ways I couldn't see. And in those moments, I understood my stepmom differently. I saw how hard it can be to love a child whose heart is still sorting through its own losses and longing.

Being a stepmom has taught me that family isn't just who you're born into, it's who you choose. And sometimes, choosing comes with both tenderness and complexity. My love for him is deep, unwavering, and real. But like adoption, blended family dynamics carry their own shadows and stretching.

Loving him expanded my empathy. It helped me see the quiet work adults are doing everywhere; choosing children who aren't biologically theirs, making space for them, and trying their best to become a safe place in a story they didn't start.

Still, the thread remains the same: belonging takes courage, from every angle.

—-

And then, a lifetime later, my two grandsons, both adopted, both miracles.

Adoption continues to weave itself through my story: beauty stitched right beside pain.

As I've aged, and become a mom and a grandmother, I've seen a new side of the story. I see the heart it takes to adopt: the courage to open your home, your routines, your future, and your heart to a child whose world has already been shaken. I see my daughter and son-in-law parent with a love that is steady and sacred. I see my grandsons, who came from hard beginnings, growing into a life held together by tenderness and intentionality.

Adoption asks something of everyone involved: the adopted child, the adopting parents, and even the siblings whose lives become braided into a story bigger than any one of them.

Through it all, I've come to understand that:
Belonging isn't automatic.
It must be tended.
Chosen.
Nurtured.
And sometimes—repaired.

PERSONAL INSIGHT

Adoption has shown me that "family" is both a gift and a responsibility. It's easy to romanticize the beauty of bringing a child into a loving home, but adoption also reveals every fracture: questions of identity, grief, displacement, fear, and the unspoken ache of children wanting to belong.

As a sibling, and later as a stepmom, I learned that chosen family, whether through adoption or blended family dynamics, affects every person involved. Roles shift, love expands but insecurities surface, and fears of abandonment can arise even when no one intends harm.

And I learned this:

The heart has many rooms.

It is possible to hold grief and gratitude at the same time.

It is possible to feel displaced and still love deeply.

It is possible to be shaped by a story that isn't "yours," and yet is part of who you are.

TAKEAWAYS

Adoption and blended families, like many of life's unexpected changes, interrupt the familiar. It stretches the heart, disrupts patterns, and opens wounds that were easier to ignore before. But they also create space for a deeper understanding of love: love that is chosen, not assumed; love that requires presence, honesty, repair, and patience.

Your story may not involve adoption or blended family dynamics, but you may know the feeling of being displaced, overlooked, or unsure of where you fit. You may know what it's like to question your belonging, or to watch others struggle with theirs.

Here's the truth:

Belonging is a journey.

It doesn't happen all at once.

And whether you are the one entering a new space or the one welcoming someone into yours, there is grace for the learning, the missteps, and the complicated emotions that come with loving people well.

SOUL NUGGETS

- *Belonging isn't given; it's cultivated.*
- *Love can expand but sometimes your heart has to stretch in uncomfortable ways first.*
- *Your place in the world is never threatened by someone else's arrival.*
- *Healing happens when truth, tenderness, and time meet.*

REFLECTION / JOURNAL PROMPTS

1. Where in your life have you felt displaced or unsure of your place in a family, relationship, or community?

2. What experiences have shaped your understanding of belonging?

3. In what ways has your heart had to stretch to love someone new, including stepchildren, adopted children, or family members entering your life through blended family dynamics?

4. What parts of your story need compassion or validation when it comes to feeling seen, chosen, or valued?

5. How has someone else's presence in your life invited you to grow in love, empathy, or understanding?

BECOMING WHOLE

WILL COST YOU

illusions,

BUT IT WILL

RETURN YOU TO

yourself.

#AThousandSmallResurrections

23

The Cost of Becoming Whole

Family

They love us, protect us, guide us, teach us, encourage us. And sometimes... they hurt us. So many of our earliest lessons come through family.

Parents are entrusted with keeping us safe, instilling beliefs, providing structure, and raising us to be good humans. It's a balancing act of love and nurturing, blended with gentle correction and necessary boundaries. Guidance can sometimes feel harsh or controlling, but more often than not, it's rooted in love.

As parents, we bring our history with us—our childhoods, our wounds, our relationship patterns. They become the blueprint we use to raise our own children. Some of us repeat the path we were shown; others choose a completely different one, rewriting the story for the next generation.

Our relationships with our parents shape everything. Science shows that our earliest memories imprint our relational patterns, our beliefs, and our sense of self.

I don't blame my parents for my life, though they certainly influenced the person I've become. I know my own children will one day say the same: that I shaped them in both good and imperfect ways. My prayer is simply that their experiences tilt more toward the good.

One of my greatest gifts is my children. Each one different in their own way. Each one teaching me something different about parenting, about life, about themselves. All four of them fill my heart with so much joy. I am so proud of them. So grateful. But motherhood hasn't been easy. Thirty-five years of raising kids, and I sometimes feel like I'm still trying to figure it out.

And now, as a grandma, I get to love on a whole new level, watching my children take what they've learned and use it to raise and shape another generation. It's beautiful to witness.

Children see the world with wonder, curiosity, joy. They're hungry to learn and grow. Their way of seeing the world lights up my soul. I think we could all use a return to that perspective.

As I've grown through my own experiences and healing, I've begun to understand the bigger picture. I've found compassion for my parents, who navigated difficult journeys of their own. Even my grandparents, who seemed to have everything figured out, carried their own quiet battles.

We're all walking a journey of discovering and uncovering who we are—within relationships, in community, and at a soul level. It's a lot.

—-

My mom and I have had our share of struggle.

What happened to me as a child shaped our relationship and scarred us both. I was guarded for many years. There were a couple seasons when we didn't speak at all. I blamed her for much of my early pain. But as I walked my healing journey, she walked hers. We found our way back to one another slowly: through highs and lows, harsh words and long silences, tears, honesty, compassion, and forgiveness.

Today, I know this: I would not be who I am or writing these words if it weren't for my mom. She has challenged me, encouraged me, seen every part of me. And when I forget who I am, she's the first one to remind me:

"Tam, you are strong.
   You are whole. You are loved. You are worthy. Your story needs to be shared.
   It's time."

—-

Writing about my dad is a little more complicated.

For most of my life, I believed he was the one man who never hurt me. I thought our relationship was the safest thing I had.

But healing doesn't just bring back memories—it brings clarity. And clarity isn't always comfortable.

For decades, I hid parts of myself from him and my stepmom. I worked hard to be the "good daughter," the easy one, the put-together one, the version they seemed to admire. I didn't want to drag the chaos of my other life into theirs. I didn't want to risk disappointing them.

What I didn't understand then was, I wasn't hiding because they demanded perfection.

I was hiding because I feared judgment and abandonment.

The same fear born on that staircase at four years old.

Throughout the years, small moments started painting the picture of reality: subtle judgments, disapproval of my choices, the way they dismissed my brother as if he didn't exist, the sting of being told design school would never amount to anything, the day my desperate request for financial help was met with a firm no. The way they used the pandemic to distance themselves from me and my sister. None of it was catastrophic, but each moment reinforced the quiet belief that love could be withdrawn.

And then came the unraveling.

When my niece's story brought buried trauma back to the surface, it stirred old wounds in all of us. My dad—once a protector of others—was overwhelmed, carrying the weight of what he hadn't known and couldn't protect me from as a child, while feeling a deep urgency to protect her. My sister and I showed up in the ways we could, but not in the ways they expected. Emotions ran high. The truth was, we were navigating something we had never been shown how to handle in a healed or healthy way.

And suddenly, their walls went up.

We were judged. Misunderstood. Cut off.

They isolated themselves from us, from our children, and even their great-grandchilden.

And the pedestal finally shattered.

It took time, tears, and truth. But here's what surprised me most:

My biggest fear came true... and I survived.
    Not just survived:
    I healed. I became whole.

The abandonment I feared my entire life happened.
    And instead of collapsing, I awakened.

It was a kind of resurrection—when the part of me shaped by fear fell away, and the part shaped by truth finally rose.

I no longer needed to perform.
    Or shrink.
    Or tiptoe.
    Or pretend.

I no longer needed to twist myself into someone acceptable to others.

For the first time, I understood:

Their withdrawal didn't break me.
    It freed me from a fear I had carried my entire life.

The space they created became sacred.

It taught me that I don't have to be chosen to be worthy.
  I don't have to be perfect to be loved.
  And I don't have to mold myself into someone else's idea of me to keep my place in their life.

I am no longer willing to conform.
  I am willing to be fully me—
  and let those who cannot receive that version gently fall away.

PERSONAL INSIGHT

Family is where our deepest wounds and deepest healing often begin. My parents shaped me in ways they never meant to; some painful, some beautiful. Loving them doesn't require denying the harm, and healing doesn't require holding onto the illusion. The truth is,
  I am not defined by what I received or didn't receive.
  I am shaped by how I've chosen to rise, repair, and rewrite the story for myself and the generations after me.

TAKEAWAYS

Your family may have shaped you, but they do not get to define you. You get to decide what patterns continue, what beliefs fall away, and what legacy you carry forward.

Healing often asks us to see our parents as imperfect humans and to see ourselves as whole, even when their love wasn't.

SOUL NUGGETS

- *You can honor where you came from without staying bound to it.*
- *Healing is the courage to tell the truth about what shaped you and to choose differently.*
- *You don't have to be chosen to be deserving of love.*
- *Sometimes the space others create becomes the room where you finally become yourself.*

REFLECTION / JOURNAL PROMPTS

1. What beliefs about love or worthiness were formed in your childhood home?

2. Which patterns from your family have you carried into adulthood, intentionally or unintentionally?

3. What truth have you avoided acknowledging about a parent or caregiver, and what would it feel like to gently name it?

4. How have your own children (or younger loved ones) inspired you to rewrite generational patterns?

5. Where have you mistaken someone's withdrawal as a reflection of your worth, and what new meaning might more healing give that story?

III

The Illumination

Broken pieces do not lose their worth.
When held with care, they bend the light.
Refraction reveals what was always there—
a brilliance made whole,
not despite the cracks, but because of them.

redemption
DOESN'T ALWAYS
RESTORE
RELATIONSHIPS,
SOMETIMES IT
restores you.

#AThousandSmallResurrections

24

The Freedom of Forgiveness

Forgiveness, for me, didn't happen all at once.

It arrived in layers—after anger had its say, after grief ran its course, after truth had been named, and after boundaries had been set.

I have forgiven my stepdad, though forgiveness did not lead to a continued relationship. I made the decision to sever ties completely—a boundary necessary for my healing.

With my mom, reconciliation became possible only after significant healing on both our parts. Our relationship today is the result of forgiveness, accountability, growth, and a shared commitment to doing better.

And as I navigate the distance with my dad and stepmom, I hold that space with compassion rather than resentment.

I see these relationships now from a higher place, one that acknowledges our shared humanity, our limitations, and the complexity of healing. Each relationship required something different of me, and each choice was made in service of my peace.

Today, I am grateful to have amicable relationships with both of my ex-husbands. That sentence alone would have felt impossible in earlier seasons of my life.

The first, is now sober and remarried. We share the joys of children, grandchildren, faith, and fond memories from our shared history. I am genuinely grateful to see him healthy, healed, and in a thriving relationship. Time, reflection, communication, forgiveness, and healing on both our parts have changed what once felt irreparably broken.

The relationship I share today with my second ex exists because of space, growth, and a shared awareness of the pain that lived between us. We actively co-parent, and the distance apart allows for a level of peace and civility that was not possible within our marriage. We engage differently. I no longer participate in toxic dynamics or cyclical fighting. I have learned when to speak, when to pause, and when to disengage. What remains is not a denial of the past, nor an illusion of safety, but a friendship shaped by compassion, clarity, and boundaries. One that honors reality while choosing peace where it is possible.

This wasn't because the past didn't matter. It mattered deeply. But healing taught me that I no longer needed to relive it.

There are others—people who've hurt me, who took advantage of my love, my empathy, my heart. I no longer hold them with bitterness. I hold them as lessons; teachers in becoming who I am now.

Not because what they did was okay.
    But because I refuse to let it consume me, harden me, or rob me of my joy and peace.

PERSONAL INSIGHT

Forgiveness is not approval. It is not always reconciliation. And it is not an invitation to re-enter harm.

Forgiveness, for me, became an act of self-liberation.

I learned that holding resentment and grudges didn't protect me—it imprisoned me. It kept my nervous system activated, my heart guarded, and my spirit tethered to moments that had already passed.

Boundaries were the bridge between pain and peace.

Some relationships were restored into something healthier. Others were released entirely. And both outcomes required forgiveness. Not for their sake, but for mine.

On a deeper, more spiritual level, I believe everyone is a child of God and is walking their own journey of discovery and soul expansion. That doesn't excuse behavior or erase accountability. It simply acknowledges that most people are carrying their own burdens, unhealed wounds, and unmet needs. Not everyone who hurts us does so with malice, though the impact still matters.

One thing I have always known about myself is that I was built with a heart of empathy.

I have always been guided by love, led with love, and able to see love in and for others, even when it wasn't returned in kind. For much of my life, I believed this was my greatest strength. What I didn't realize was how often my empathy excluded me. I gave love freely, sometimes at the expense of my own well-being, mistaking self-abandonment for selflessness.

Healing has taught me that love was never meant to bypass me.

Today, my journey includes a sacred pause. A moment where I ask myself, *How can I love and forgive others while loving and forgiving myself too?* That pause has changed everything. It has allowed me to remain compassionate without overextending, present without depletion, and open-hearted without neglecting myself. When empathy includes self-love, it becomes sustainable. And from that place, peace is not only possible, it's protected.

Forgiveness allowed me to see clearly without minimizing truth.

And through it all, I came to understand this:
God does not force pain upon us, but He does redeem it.

What was meant to break me became what refined me.
What wounded me became what awakened compassion.
What nearly hardened my heart became the place where grace took root.

I want to be clear: I am not saying or implying that healing always leads to reconnection, restored relationships, or healthy communication. Each situation is deeply personal, complex, and unique.
For some, forgiveness may mean distance, silence, or permanent boundaries. For others, it may mean limited or structured contact. And for some, reconciliation is neither safe nor wise. Healing does not

follow a single formula, and forgiveness does not require continued access to those who caused harm.

TAKEAWAYS

Forgiveness may look different in your life than it does in mine, and that's okay.

You are not required to stay in relationship with someone who harmed you.

You are not required to explain your healing to anyone.

You are not required to rush forgiveness before your body, heart, and spirit are ready.

What you are invited to do is loosen the grip resentment has on you.

Forgiveness is not about restoring the past; it's about reclaiming your present.

When you forgive, you choose peace over poison. You choose softness without surrendering strength. You choose to trust that God can carry what you no longer need to hold.

We are all stardust of the same universe; created by the same God, connected, growing one another for the collective good. And somehow, in ways only God can orchestrate, even the hardest chapters are woven into redemption.

"And we know that God causes everything to work together for the good of

those who love God and are called according to His purpose for them."
— Romans 8:28 (NLT)

SOUL NUGGETS

- *Forgiveness is about freedom, not fairness.*
- *Boundaries are not bitterness, they are wisdom.*
- *You don't heal by forgetting, you heal by releasing.*
- *Love that includes you is not selfish; it's sustainable.*

REFLECTION / JOURNAL PROMPTS

1. What form might forgiveness take for you: reconnection, limited contact, distance, or walking away? Why does that feel right for where you are today?

2. If forgiveness were not about the other person, but about your own freedom, what would you be ready to release? What resentments, narratives, or emotional weights are you still carrying that no longer serve your healing?

3. Imagine what peace might feel like in your body if forgiveness began to replace anger, bitterness, or unresolved pain. Where would you notice the shift first: your breath, your thoughts, your relationships, your sense of self?

4. What boundaries would need to be in place for forgiveness to feel safe and sustainable in your life?

5. How can empathy and self-love coexist more fully in you? What might change if compassion included you as deeply as it includes others?

RESOURCE NOTE: FORGIVENESS & SAFETY

Forgiveness is often misunderstood—especially in the context of abuse, trauma, or long-term harm. Forgiving someone does not mean excusing their behavior, minimizing the impact, or placing yourself back in unsafe situations.

If you have experienced emotional, physical, sexual, or psychological abuse, healing may require distance, no contact, or the support of a therapist, advocate, or trusted community. Choosing safety, boundaries, or silence is not bitterness, it is wisdom.

Forgiveness is an internal process that unfolds in its own time. It cannot be forced, rushed, or demanded by others or by faith. God is not dishonored by your need for protection, clarity, or space.

If you are navigating forgiveness alongside trauma, consider seeking support through trauma-informed counseling, domestic violence or sexual assault advocacy organizations, or faith-based counselors trained in abuse recovery. Healing is not meant to be done alone.

I invite you to visit the **Resources for Support & Healing** section at the back of this book.

FAITH

IS A

journey,

NOT A

moment.

#AThousandSmallResurrections

25

Faith Full Circle

I've always had a strong faith—an inner knowing that there was something bigger than me. A life force beyond my understanding. It was never about religion. I don't recall an earlier moment of "giving my life to Jesus." I just always knew He was there.

What I can recall are the countless drop-to-my-knees moments when the weight of heartbreak, secrets, and pain became too heavy to carry alone. Those were the moments I cried out for help. I surrendered. And every time, in one way or another, my prayers were answered.

Sometimes it looked like my best friend calling right after I'd prayed for guidance.

Other times, it was an unexplainable peace washing over my body as I prayed for comfort before heart surgery, or strength when I was weary.

The job offer arriving days after I released my fears about finances to God.

The words I begged for to calm my child's anxious heart.

Whenever I questioned if I was on the right path, or wondered if I was truly alone, signs would appear to remind me I wasn't. Repeating numbers. Song lyrics speaking directly to my heart. Unexpected words of encouragement. And after heart surgery, hearts began appearing everywhere: in clouds, rocks, coffee spills, even shadows. Tiny reminders that love was always near.

However the message arrived, it was always on time and said the same thing:

There is something greater.

There is a divine Creator who listens, who sees, who loves, and who stays—even when no one else does.

And looking back now, I can see that each of those moments weren't just guidance or comfort—they were resurrections in disguise. Tiny ways God kept breathing life back into the parts of me I thought were gone.

Each answered prayer, each whisper of peace, each perfectly timed sign was a gentle rising, evidence that nothing in me was too broken for God to restore.

— -

For years, I felt the pull to be water baptized as an adult. But fear always held me back. The idea of standing before others and publicly professing my faith felt vulnerable and overwhelming. So I tucked the desire away, quietly in my heart.

My adult children had been visiting a local church for awhile and often shared how deeply the messages resonated with them. One Sunday, during COVID, curiosity nudged me to join an online service. Week after week, I found myself moved, not just by the sermons, but by how personally they seemed to speak to me.

Then one morning, the pastor announced an upcoming water baptism. My heart leapt. For the first time, I didn't feel afraid—I felt ready. Excited, even. The thought of outwardly expressing what had always been inwardly true filled me with joy. When my oldest son mentioned he was considering being baptized too, I couldn't imagine a more meaningful experience to share.

But as the day approached, doubts crept in. Not about my faith, but about the location. I had never attended this church in person. I had attended a few churches over the years, but none had truly felt like home. I wondered if maybe I should wait, if perhaps this sacred step should happen somewhere more familiar.

So I decided to go to a midweek worship night, to feel the call on my heart in person.

Driving there, I wasn't paying close attention to the directions. It wasn't until I turned into the parking lot that my breath caught in my throat.

I knew this place.

The church looked modern and ordinary on the outside, but a section of the building—its doors, the layout, the curve of the lot—hit me with the force of memory.

This wasn't just any church.

This was my old elementary school.

And just beyond it, down the short, curved road, stood the house. *The house from my childhood.* The house tied to my nightmare. The driveway that highlighted my internal pain of silence, of being haunted, chased, and unable to escape.

I sat in my car, frozen, staring at the past standing directly in front of me. Then, deep within my spirit, I heard it:

"Yes. This is exactly where I'm calling you to be. I'm bringing you back to set you free."

I broke. I sobbed until I couldn't breathe. Grief, memory, and grace all collided as I walked inside that building and worshiped there for the first time.

Of course it had to be *here.*

Of course my redemption would begin in the same place where my innocence had been stolen.

Of course God would bring healing to the exact ground where wounding had begun.

That next Sunday, I stood beside my son, publicly declaring my faith, yes, but also a private moment of healing. With water cascading over me I was made new.

It was a homecoming—not to the house, but to my soul and to my Creator.

A reclaiming of sacred ground.

A full-circle miracle only God could orchestrate.

PERSONAL INSIGHT

Sometimes healing doesn't look like escaping the past, it looks like being led straight back to it, but this time with love instead of fear. I never imagined that the road that once led to pain would someday guide me toward peace. But that's how grace works: it loops back, tenderly rewriting the story where it first began.

Standing in that water, I felt the weight of decades lift; not just from my shoulders, but from that little girl's heart. The one who once stood in that driveway, afraid and unseen. She was finally safe. Finally free.

Because God doesn't just heal what was broken;
    He restores what was lost.
    And when we surrender—*truly surrender*—
    He leads us back to the places we were first wounded,
    so we can see them through the eyes of redemption.

TAKEAWAYS

Faith isn't a single moment; it's a series of invitations. God meets us in our breaking points, our quiet questions, and our small everyday steps forward.

Healing often brings us back to old places with new strength. You aren't the same person who was hurt there; redemption lets you return empowered, protected, and held.

God speaks through alignment as much as miracles. Signs, synchronicities, symbols, and small unexpected moments are not coincidences, they are conversations.

Resurrection isn't always dramatic or instantaneous. Sometimes it's one small rising after another as God breathes life back into the places where we once felt empty, lost, or undone.

Your healing, your faith, and your becoming are all built on quiet resurrections. Pay attention to them. They're the proof that God is restoring you in real time.

SOUL NUGGETS

- *Faith doesn't demand perfection; it invites trust.*
- *What once wounded you can become the ground where restoration begins.*
- *Surrender isn't losing control; it's stepping into divine alignment.*
- *The same God who met you in your pain now leads you into your healing.*

REFLECTION / JOURNAL PROMPTS

1. Where have you experienced small resurrections in your life: moments where something in you quietly came back to life?

2. What signs, synchronicities or "God winks" have shown you that you are being guided, held, or renewed?

3. True surrender isn't giving up; it's giving over. What burden, fear, or unanswered question might you need to place in divine hands today?

4. Healing often means revisiting the very spaces or memories that once felt unbearable but with new strength, truth, and faith. What part of your story are you ready to reclaim as holy?

5. Faith isn't always found in one defining moment. Sometimes, it's something you've known all along quietly carrying you through. How might that look like for you?

EVERY

echo

CARRIES A

new way

TO LOVE YOURSELF

AND OTHERS.

#AThousandSmallResurrections

26

Echos & Awakenings

After my second marriage ended, I swore I was done with relationships. I meant it. I was exhausted, bruised, and convinced that companionship wasn't worth the cost. But humans are wired for connection. Eventually, I realized I still desired companionship.

However, dating in your fifties is something no one prepares you for. Certainly not after two marriages, heartbreak after heartbreak, and years of healing work you once believed would "finish the job."

It's not always a handful of therapy sessions, a journal full of revelations, a self-help book, or a weekend retreat that magically removes heartbreak or trauma from the body. Healing tends to be a lifelong relationship with yourself—one that deepens with each season, each trigger, each new experience that asks you to look inward.

Healing taught me to see myself with clarity—but dating?
   Dating has been its own kind of teacher.

The digital age of dating is a wild landscape: apps with instant swipes, inappropriate messages, ghosting, situationships, attachment styles tossed around like personality types, and online community groups warning women about local predators and cheaters. You need a strong sense of self if you attempt to navigate the jungle that is the dating scene today.

And so here I am—stepping into new territory.
Curiously. Cautiously. Authentically.

What has surprised me most isn't the men I've met and gotten to know, but the echoes: faint reverberations of earlier wounds that have shown up in familiar ways.
Not as loud as they used to be.
Not as devastating.
But still present enough to remind me that my body remembers.

These echoes have become teachers.
And in their own way, each echo has been rising, an awakening of a part of me I once ignored in order to survive.

Each encounter, each connection, has illuminated something within me that still needs tending. A trigger I hadn't noticed. A pattern I hadn't broken. A piece of my heart that still needed gentleness.

I've learned to pause.
To breathe.
To listen to my body.
To question the sensation behind the anxiety instead of abandoning myself.

Because here is the truth I learned the hard way: The love I crave from others is simply the reflection of the love that awakens in me when I care for someone. The problem has been that I often traded pieces of myself for that feeling.

The more I reach outward, the further I drifted from myself.

Dating, unexpectedly, has become another form of healing. Not because I'm broken, but because it shows me where I still need to return home.

I've noticed things about myself:
That I still sometimes look for validation from others.
That I chase connection because I think it will make me happier.
That I feel sexy and alive when someone desires me.
That I get disappointed when they don't measure up to my expectations.
That I still abandon myself in subtle ways.

But I've also noticed what is true:
I am whole on my own.
I am strongest when I listen to my intuition.
My body speaks to me—and I honor her now.
I feel most alive when I am connected to my own soul.
I thrive when I protect my peace.

And while I still have expectations of others in my relationships, I am learning to meet myself first.

Dating has revealed and reminded me of my need for soulful connection, safety, creativity, friendship, stability, and soul expansion. Each person on this journey has held up a mirror to a different part of me, both the wounded and the awakened.

Every encounter has led me back to the same place: boundary setting, staying centered, and returning home to myself.

Healing has shown me that resurrection rarely comes in a single moment. It often arrives quietly, in a shifted perspective, a boundary honored, a moment when I choose myself again. A gentle, continuous rising. A small resurrection every time I return to my truth.

PERSONAL INSIGHT

Dating hasn't just taught me about those I've connected with, it's also teaching me about me.

It's revealing where echoes of old wounds still whisper, where I still seek validation, and where I still sometimes abandon myself. It has shown me that healing isn't about being flawless before letting someone in, it's about recognizing my patterns, honoring my intuition, regulating my nervous system, and choosing myself first every time.

The spiritual awakening isn't simply in finding love again; it is in becoming the woman who refuses to lose herself in the process.

This chapter of my life is less about romance and more about rising into the kind of self-trust that can hold me steady in love or in solitude.

TAKEAWAYS

Dating, no matter what stage of life you're in, is not about finding someone perfect or proving your worth. It's about showing up as your whole self, noticing the echoes of your past, and choosing to respond with awareness rather than old patterns.

Your healing doesn't disqualify you from love; it equips you for it.
When you listen to your intuition, honor your boundaries, and stay rooted in your truth, dating becomes less about being chosen and more about choosing what aligns with your peace, your purpose, and your soul.

This season isn't about remaking yourself for love. It's about rising into the woman love must meet at your level.

SOUL NUGGETS

- *Every trigger is an echo, not a failure. An invitation, not a setback.*
- *The love you seek from others is a reflection of the love you're learning to give yourself.*
- *You don't need someone to complete you; you need someone who honors the completeness you already carry.*
- *Your intuition is your safest home. You body is your wisest guide.*

REFLECTION / JOURNAL PROMPTS

1. What echoes from past relationships still show up for you when seeking connection?

2. When you feel triggered, what sensations does your body use to get your attention?

3. What expectations do you place on others that are actually unmet needs within yourself?

4. What qualities do you want in a partner and which of those qualities are you cultivating within yourself?

223

healing

PAINTS

THE WORLD

IN

technicolor.

#AThousandSmallResurrections

27

A Passport to My Heart

Before I Ever Arrived

Before I ever set foot on her streets, I had already lived in Paris.

In my mind, I strolled along cobblestone paths with a sketchbook tucked under my arm, stopping at small cafés where time slowed. I painted shutters and grand doorways, journaled beneath striped awnings, and lingered in art museums where beauty hummed quietly through the halls. I imagined myself dressed like the women I saw in old time movies; effortless, expressive, classic.

I watched lovers kiss beneath the Eiffel Tower as it twinkled against the night sky, its reflection dancing along the Seine. I breathed in espresso and rain and felt, somehow, that the city knew me. Paris wasn't just a place I wanted to visit—it was a place my soul recognized.

I was fifteen when that dream took hold.

Paris became my refuge during one of the hardest seasons of my life.

When home didn't feel safe. When love felt conditional. When I waited by the phone for a call that never came, convincing myself that longing was the same as love. Instead of going out with friends, I escaped inward, to the dreamy streets of Paris, where beauty existed freely and art was allowed to breathe.

It felt as though I had lived a lifetime there already.

As though the city had been holding a version of me until I was ready to arrive.

When I started high school, I enrolled in French class, advanced art, and architectural design. I was preparing for a life I didn't yet have, but deeply believed I would someday live. I loved the details: the symmetry of French architecture, the old-world charm, the art, the beauty, and of course, the Eiffel Tower; where romance unfolded nightly beneath her glowing lights.

And then—life happened.

There was always a reason not to go. Money. Marriage. Children. Time. Partners whose visions for vacation looked nothing like mine. The dream dimmed, but it never disappeared.

Years later, after seasons of hardship, healing, standing up for myself, rebuilding, and eventually living solo again, a moment arrived— quiet but unmistakable. For the first time, the excuses felt thinner than the longing.

And then my daughter asked a simple question that undid every excuse I had ever made:

"So, are you finally going to take that trip to Paris you've always talked about?"

Something clicked.
Why *not* now?

This was my time.
No compromises.
No waiting.
No shrinking.

— -

Why This Journey Called Me

Paris was the heartbeat of the dream, but Italy was the echo.

Florence called to the artist in me; the part that believes beauty is sacred. I wandered through streets taking in its old-world charm and rich history with reverence. Where the weathered textures and tarnished patinas of centuries-old buildings are softened by vines and flowers, timeless and effortlessly beautiful. The colors alone felt like home: terracottas, deep burgundies, sunlit golds, and lush greens. It was like a quiet conversation between the past and my present becoming.

Tuscany invited slowness. Golden hills rolled endlessly beneath wide skies, vineyards stretching like brushstrokes across the land. I tasted wine warmed by the sun, lingering on my tongue; earthy, full-bodied, patient. Meals unfolded unhurriedly: crusty bread torn by hand, olive oil shimmering, laughter drifting through open windows. It reminded me that life is meant to be savored, not rushed.

The Cinque Terre drew me in with its bold colors and captivating views. Villages painted in joyful defiance, clinging to cliffs above the sea. The scent of salt hung in the air as waves crashed rhythmically below, steady and faithful. I watched the light shift across the water, felt the wind on my skin, and recognized myself there—shaped by storms, yet still choosing vibrancy. The sunset melting into the sea was nothing short of spectacular. As if God had painted it just for me.

And Rome, layered, ancient, and eternal, offered itself in fragments and feasts. Cobblestones worn smooth by centuries. Fountains murmuring secrets. The taste of pasta, vino and tiramisu late into the evening, rich and indulgent, as twilight softened the city. History breathed all around me, ruin and glory intertwined, proof that nothing meaningful escapes time, and everything sacred endures.

This wasn't a random itinerary.
  It was a pilgrimage.

Each place awakened a different part of me—the dreamer, the artist, the woman learning to linger, the survivor who still believes in beauty.

— -

The Journey Itself

I traveled solo not because I had no one to come with me, but because I was finally ready to listen to the call of my soul.

Solo travel became an act of self-trust. I moved at the pace of my intuition. I followed what sparked joy without negotiating or explaining. There was no performance. No permission needed. Just presence.

This trip wasn't about escape.

It was about arrival.

It was a reclamation of my soul—a romantic journey for one, a long-overdue love affair with myself. Every experience, every moment, became a gift to the versions of me who once stayed small, dimmed her light, or molded herself into what others needed her to be.

Healing changes the way you experience the world.
  Colors deepen.
  Flavors linger.
  Moments stretch wide.

The storms you survive make the rainbows unmistakably more vibrant.

Standing beneath the Eiffel Tower on my birthday, celebrating another year of life, love, and becoming, I realized something profound: my lived experiences had sharpened my capacity for joy. Everything felt magnified. Sacred. Full.

This trip didn't change me.
  It revealed me.

PERSONAL INSIGHT

Life is meant to be experienced in its fullest expression. Healing paints the world in technicolor. Everything becomes more vibrant.

Solo travel opens a portal; a space where you see yourself as more expansive, creative, and free.

I wasn't lonely. I was deeply attuned.

When you heal, when you love yourself fully, you don't wait for life to begin.
    You meet it; open-hearted and awake.

There really is heaven on earth.
    Sometimes it looks like Paris at dusk.
    Sometimes like sun-soaked hills in Tuscany.
    Sometimes like realizing you are finally home within yourself.

TAKEAWAYS

There is a dream inside you that has survived every season of your life.
    It didn't disappear because it couldn't; it was waiting.

You don't need permission to live it.
    You don't need perfect timing, a partner, or a plan.
    You only need the courage to say yes to yourself.

Take the trip. Start the project. Follow the nudge.

The beauty you're longing for is already reaching for you.

SOUL NUGGETS

- *Some dreams don't fade, they wait for healing.*
- *Joy becomes more vibrant after darkness.*
- *Solo does not mean alone; it means sovereign.*
- *When you choose yourself, the world opens.*

REFLECTION / JOURNAL PROMPTS

1. What dream has lived quietly in your heart for years?

2. Where have you delayed joy while waiting for "someday"?

3. How has your healing changed the way you experience beauty?

4. What would a love affair with yourself look like right now?

5. Where is your soul inviting you to go next?

YOUR HEALING, YOUR POWER, YOUR LIGHT—

IT'S BEEN THERE *all along.*

#AThousandSmallResurrections

28

Coming Home to Myself

The Revelation that took me decades to figure out: *I Am the Key*

It was me all along.

Just like Dorothy in *The Wizard of Oz*, I set out on a journey searching for answers—believing someone else held the wisdom, the fix, the healing, the love, the way home. Along the way, I met people who taught me more about compassion, courage, and truth. And like Dorothy, I faced obstacles that tested me, stretched me, and sometimes broke me open.

Each challenge I faced was like a small death—of old beliefs, fears, or limitations—only for me to rise again stronger, clearer, and closer to home.

But in the end, the revelation was clear:
   The power to return home—to myself, to my spirit—had been within me all along.

The Woman Behind the Curtain: Seeing Myself Clearly at Last

My hardships, my silence, my searching, and ultimately my healing, pulled back the curtain to reveal that:

My inner knowing is my connection to my soul, to Source.

Everything and everyone I ever sought outside of myself was always inside me.

Self-love and acceptance are the ultimate key to unlocking true peace, overwhelming joy, and unconditional love.

Just like the moon, I move through phases of light and darkness, and everything in between. My brightness may not always appear the same, but I am always whole.

I realize that I am my biggest cheerleader, my harshest critic, my best friend, or my worst enemy. The one who loves me best, but can also hurt me most. How I treat her, how I speak to her, how I listen to her, is a reflection of my healing journey.

In a place of compassion and introspection, what I know to be true about all the versions of myself is:

I understand her—her quirks, her insecurities, her pain, her heart.

Her precious heart loves deeply and only wants to be seen, understood, and loved unconditionally.

Yes, she is emotional, and that is beautiful, because it reflects her soul.

Yes, she can be larger than life when she allows her true self to shine.

I get her.

I love her, in all her moments, in all her mess, and all her glory.

She's not too much, too bright, or too feeling.

She's exactly as she was meant to be.

The world has tried to dim her light again and again,
   but each time it did, it only gave her more fuel to ignite a brighter flame.

She always rises—higher, brighter, lighter—resurrecting her spirit with every lesson learned, every scar transformed into wisdom.
   She is unstoppable.

And so, I will do my best to listen to her.
   See her.
   Respect her.
   Fight for her.
   Honor her.

—-

The Journey Back to My Power

I'm not just the stories within these pages, but a kaleidoscope of experiences, relationships, lessons, and awakenings, each one shaping me into who I am today.

What happened to me doesn't define me. It has refined me.

I am not the victim, the failed wife, the imperfect daughter, the helpless mother, or the defective heart patient.

I am so much more.

My spirit is too vast, too radiant to be confined by labels or boxes.

It's the lessons uncovered, the grace received, and the growth I've fought for that have made me who I am, and who I am still becoming.

Each heartbreak, each triumph, each act of self-love has been a quiet resurrection, bringing me back to my fullest self again and again.

TAKEAWAYS

You have always held the key. Every answer you've searched for, every piece of love you've tried to earn, every moment you've felt lost has been guiding you back to yourself. Back to your Source.

The journey is not about becoming someone new; it's about remembering who you've always been. When you honor your intuition, extend compassion to your past selves, and choose to overcome what hurt you, you reclaim your power.

Choosing to rise from what tried to break you is your daily resurrection: proof that your light cannot be dimmed, your spirit cannot be defeated.

To wax and wane like the moon is to grow, expand, and brighten, while also being able to rest, retreat, or soften without losing yourself. Understanding that your light doesn't disappear; it changes. Remaining whole the entire time.

Reminding you of your truth:
You are whole, worthy, and luminous right now, as you are.

SOUL NUGGETS

- *Coming home to yourself is not a destination; it's a daily devotion.*
- *You are not lost; you are learning to listen.*
- *Wholeness isn't something you find; it's something you remember.*
- *Your inner wisdom has been speaking; healing is learning to hear it.*

REFLECTION / JOURNAL PROMPTS

1. Where in your own story have you searched for answers outside yourself?

2. What version of you still needs compassion, forgiveness, or understanding?

3. Where does your inner voice feel the quietest and what might help hear her more clearly?

4. What truths about yourself have you outgrown, and what new truths are you stepping into?

5. Where in your life have you risen from what once felt like an ending, and how can you honor that rebirth today?

FROM
BROKENNESS TO
brilliance,
EVERY CHOICE
TO RISE IS
sacred.

#AThousandSmallResurrections

29

The Alchemy of Healing

What I've come to understand is that healing is not something done *to* us, it is something awakened *in* us.

True healing begins inside. In the still, unseen places of the soul.

It begins with **surrender.**
The quieting of your mind and the softening of your heart.
The willingness to pause long enough to hear the still, small voice of your soul, the divine whisper that dwells within you.

In that stillness, and introspection, you discover something sacred:
It was you all along.
The love you seek.
The acceptance you crave.
The strength and certainty you once searched for in others:
they have always been within you.
You hold the power to heal.
You hold the key to your freedom.

Healing comes through **release.**

Letting go of the stories, the shadows, the weight you've carried far too long. The lies you've told yourself.

The guilt. The shame. The "not enoughs."

When you release them, you become lighter. Freer.

More open to love—for yourself, and for the world around you.

And as your heart opens, so does your capacity to heal.

This is where **compassion** blooms.

Where you give grace to older versions of you.

Where empathy for others blossoms.

Where humanness meets humanness.

Where your light becomes a guide for someone else's darkness.

Healing deepens through **connection.**

Through listening, sharing, expressing, and speaking your truth.

When we share our stories, we break the illusion of isolation.

We begin to live with more **authenticity**.

No longer afraid to be seen as flawed or imperfect.

We remind one another that we are not alone.

This—the courage to love, to connect, to be seen—is the alchemy of healing.

Surrender, release, compassion, connection, authenticity: these are not just steps. They are the sacred elements of transformation. The chemistry by which brokenness transmutes into brilliance.

The process by which your soul remembers who it has always been.

PERSONAL INSIGHT

I used to think resurrection was one miraculous moment; a sudden, shining breakthrough, a single lift from darkness into light.

But now I know:
Resurrection is every breath we choose after loss.
Every truth we speak.
Every boundary we set.
Every time we rise again.

These are the thousand small resurrections that brought me home to myself.

They are not only proof of survival, but evidence of thriving. The alchemy of healing transforms grief into wisdom, heartbreak into compassion, pain into power.

TAKEAWAYS

Healing is both an inward journey and an outward offering.
It begins in stillness, in learning to sit with your pain instead of running from it.
From that stillness comes revelation; a remembering of who you truly are.

When you return to your center, your presence becomes medicine for yourself and for others. Every act of self-honoring, every moment of rising, every choice to be authentic is a resurrection of your spirit.

Your healing is your gift. Your light is your legacy.

SOUL NUGGETS

- *Healing begins in stillness but expands through connection.*
- *Surrender and release create the soil for your soul to bloom.*
- *When you remember your own light, you become a source of hope and healing for others.*
- *Authenticity is the alchemy that transforms brokenness into brilliance.*

REFLECTION / JOURNAL PROMPTS

1. What are you being called to surrender right now?

2. What truth within you is ready to be remembered?

3. What stories, beliefs, or lies are you ready to release so you can make room for healing?

4. How might your own healing ripple outward through compassion, connection, or truth-telling?

5. Which actions or choices can you take today that honor your soul and reflect resurrection of your spirit?

YOUR PAIN

IS THE

cocoon.

YOUR

resurrection

IS WAITING.

#AThousandSmallResurrections

30

The Sacred In-Between

Facing the Ache: The Invitation to Transform

To the beautiful soul reading these words, I say this as gently as I can and with the utmost love: It's time to put it down.

Stop carrying the pain. The stories you've held on to about your past or your current situation. The narratives about your worth, your circumstances, your relationships. Stop performing. Stop hiding. Stop keeping the truest, most radiant version of your soul behind masks and false truths.

Your soul came here to learn, to grow, to experience. Every heartbreak, every secret, every wound has served its purpose. They have challenged you, stretched you, taught you, and shaped you.

But now—it's time to set her free.

Listen to your inner being. She's never failed you and she never will. Take the time to heal. Grow. Do what sets your soul on fire. Take the trip you've been dreaming of. Write the book. Take the class. Speak your truth.

Your people will still love you. And if they don't—they weren't meant to. This lifetime is fleeting. Don't waste another day holding what isn't yours to carry.

— -

The Cocoon: Pain as Preparation

Think of the caterpillar in its cocoon. The transformation isn't comfortable. It's not instantaneous. It's not gentle. It's a quiet, slow, unseen labor that leads to rebirth.

Your inner work—the willingness to face what has been hidden—is your cocoon from which healing emerges. This is your sacred growing season. The part nobody talks about. The part skipped over in social posts. The part that makes you cry, that stretches you, that tests your endurance.

Healing happens in the in-between: the awkward, messy, uncertain spaces where transformation is quietly occurring. This is where resurrection begins: in the small choices to rise, to stay, to sit with what is, and to trust what will be.

This season is not punishment, it's preparation.

Strong winds will either topple a tree or force its roots to dig deeper. Just like storms teach trees to grow roots in order to anchor them more firmly into the earth, your hardships work the same way.

The process doesn't expose weakness; it builds strength.

—-

The Fragmented Mirror: Seeing Yourself Fully

I challenge you to be open to seeing your reflection. To loving her in the vulnerable moments as you gaze into her soul.

You are a kaleidoscope of fragmented mirrors. Broken shards, collected, tended, and gently put back together. Each piece bouncing light onto the next, reflecting a spectrum of color so vivid, so uniquely yours.

Your brokenness is not a mark of failure. It's a prism that makes your light shine brighter. Every shard is a piece of your resurrection story—proof that you endured, that you rose, that you returned home to yourself.

PERSONAL INSIGHT

Healing is never a straight line. It's not a single event; it is a series of deaths and resurrections. The old versions of yourself, the beliefs that limited you, the fear that held you back, the pain you thought would break you, must first fall away. Only then can your soul emerge renewed, radiant, and whole.

The sacred in-between is not a pause; it is preparation. It is where your roots grow deep, where your spirit strengthens, and where your resurrection takes shape.

TAKEAWAYS

Pain is preparation, not punishment.

The hardest seasons often yield the deepest growth.

True transformation requires sitting with discomfort, leaning into the ache, and trusting the process.

Resurrection—emerging stronger, freer, and more whole—is the reward of your faithful endurance.

SOUL NUGGETS

- *Your cocoon is sacred; your wings are waiting.*
- *Transformation requires patience, presence, and courage.*
- *Every broken piece of you reflects the light you carry.*
- *The in-between is where your roots deepen, your soul strengthens, and your brilliance is born.*

REFLECTION / JOURNAL PROMPTS

1. Where in your life have you resisted sitting with discomfort and what might happen if you allowed it?

2. How can you honor the "in-between" seasons as part of your sacred transformation?

3. Which parts of your past or self need to be lovingly acknowledged before they can be resurrected into wholeness?

YOU ARE

THE

author

OF YOUR

becoming.

#AThousandSmallResurrections

31

The Great Story of You

To All the Versions of Me—and to You:

I'm so proud of you for doing your best to be okay. I'm proud of you for waking up every day and choosing to love *you*.

I know some of your yesterdays were really hard. But look at how far you've come. You've grown so much. You're going to get through what you're currently going through.

Keep fighting for yourself. You're someone worth fighting for.

Do it for you—because every beat of your heart is calling you in this direction.
   Because every cell of your being is awakening.
   Because your soul knows the way.

You are worthy of your wildest dreams. Dare to dream. Dare to create. Dare to love. Dare to share. Dare to inspire.

You deserve all the good that exists on the other side of healing.

What has happened in your life is not random. It is the great story of *you*.

—-

Your Pain Is Not in Vain

Do not surrender your power to the shadows. They will rob you of joy, love, and peace. Instead, stand bold and unafraid. Your truth will light the way forward.

It only takes a spark to illuminate the path, and you already carry that sacred spark within you.

Do not fear what lies ahead. You hold the key—and remembering who you are will set you free.
　　Peace is possible.
　　Hope carries infinite power.
　　Love is your greatest strength.

Be fearless in your pursuit of joy, in creating the life you deserve, and in shining your unique light.

You are not alone, and your struggles are not in vain. They are shaping you, elevating your consciousness, and transforming your pain into purpose.

Shine your light boldly into the world.

—-

My Desire for You

To my beautiful reader, my hope is that you find peace, happiness, joy, clarity, and a renewed sense of purpose.

That you discover your inner power.

That when you face heartbreak, hardship, trauma or repeating patterns, you see them. Recognize them. And stop them. Healing generational trauma.

That you decide: Enough is enough. You are no longer a victim.

That you realize you are the author of your becoming.

You are the author of the great story of you.

And every choice to rise, every small victory, every act of self-love— these are your thousand small resurrections, leading you closer to the fullest version of yourself.

TAKEAWAYS

Your story, no matter how messy, painful, or uncertain, is unfolding with purpose.

Every version of you has carried wisdom, courage, and light to this moment.

Healing is not a single moment, but a series of small resurrections; one choice, one breath, one truth at a time.

You do not need to have it all figured out. Showing up for yourself is enough.

Your life is sacred, and the world needs the light only you can bring.

SOUL NUGGETS

- *You are not broken; you are a kaleidoscope of a thousand small resurrections.*
- *Every pain you've endured has prepared you for the beauty, joy, and peace you now claim.*
- *Healing is cumulative: the quiet victories, the daily choices, the self-love, all lead to resurrection.*
- *Your story matters. Your presence matters. Your light matters.*

REFLECTION / JOURNAL PROMPTS

1. Which of your " small resurrections" are you most proud of?

2. How can you celebrate your resilience and growth today?

3. What narrative about yourself are you ready to release so your story can fully shine?

255

4. How might your life, with all its lessons and triumphs, inspire someone else?

HEALING

IS NOT A

MOMENT, IT'S A

thousand

SMALL

resurrections.

#AThousandSmallResurrections

32

A Whisper to Your Soul

For every version of yourself that you've loved and lost,
   for every small fracture that became a prism of light,
   for every tear, every scar, every quiet victory—
   you are here. You have risen. Again and again.

Let the memory of pain be your teacher,
   not your captor.
   Let the echoes of fear remind you of your courage.
   Let every heartbreak be a doorway,
   and every stumble, a step toward grace.

You have learned the art of resurrection.
   Not once. Not in a moment.
   But a thousand times, in a thousand ways,
   with every choice to stand, to breathe, to love,
   to return to yourself.

Carry your light gently, fiercely, beautifully.
There is beauty in the breaking, wisdom in the ache,
and redemption in every small, deliberate rise.

The story of your life is sacred,
but the story of you—your heart, your soul, your becoming—
is a masterpiece of infinite worth.

So rise, beautiful.
Rise with tenderness and fire.
Rise with gratitude for all you have survived.
Rise with audacity for all that awaits you.

Because you are whole,
you are luminous,
you are a thousand small resurrections made visible.

And this—this is just the beginning.

Resources for Support & Healing

Because none of us are meant to carry this alone.

###

Resources Disclaimer

The resources listed in this section are provided for informational purposes only and were accurate at the time of publication. This book does not provide medical, legal, psychological, or therapeutic advice. Laws, services, and contact information may change over time, so please verify details directly through official websites.

If you are in immediate danger or experiencing a medical or mental health emergency, call 911 (in the United States) or your local emergency number.

Seeking help is a courageous step. Professional support can provide personalized guidance tailored to your unique situation.

The stories shared in this book touch on experiences that many carry quietly, sometimes for years. If anything you've read stirred memories, emotions, or questions, support is available. You deserve care, understanding, and help on your own terms and timeline.

If you're wondering whether your experience "counts" or is "bad enough" to seek help, it does.

You are allowed to ask for support.
You are allowed to need help.
You are allowed to heal.

This book was never meant to be the end of the conversation. Support is part of healing.

SEXUAL ABUSE / ASSAULT / HARASSMENT

If you've experienced sexual abuse, assault, harassment, or any form of unwanted sexual misconduct, what happened to you was not your fault.

Confidential support is available.

United States

- **RAINN** (National sexual assault hotline)
  Call: 800-656-HOPE (4673)
  Website: RAINN.org
  Available 24/7 by phone or online chat

- **Love Is Respect** (Dating abuse & coercion)
  Call: 866-331-9474
  Text: LOVEIS to 22522
  Website: LoveIsRespect.org

- **Crisis Text Line**
  Text: STRENGTH to 741-741

International

- Find local trusted resources at: **Findahelpline.com**

Healing is not linear. You are allowed to move at your own pace. You are allowed to reclaim your body, your voice, and your story.

WORKPLACE SEXUAL HARASSMENT

If you've experienced sexual harassment at work or are unsure whether behavior crossed the line, you have rights.

Organizations can help you understand your options and next steps.

United States

- **Equal Employment Opportunity Commission (EEOC)**
  Website: EEOC.gov
  Information on workplace rights and how to file a charge

- **HarassmentHelp.org**
  Confidential guidance and support

- **Equality Rights Advocates (ERA)**
  Free legal advice and counseling
  Call: 1-800-839-4372

Laws vary by state and country. If you are outside the U.S., contact your local labor or human rights commission.

You deserve to feel safe and respected at work.

SUICIDE / SUICIDAL THOUGHTS / EMOTIONAL CRISIS

If you or someone you love is struggling with thoughts of self-harm or suicide, immediate and confidential support is available.

United States

- **988 Suicide & Crisis Lifeline**
  Call or text: 988
  Available 24/7

International

- **Findahelpline.com** connects you to local crisis support in your country

Immediate danger

- **Call 911** (U.S.) or your local emergency number

Reaching out is not a sign of weakness—it is a courageous act of hope.

ADDICTION (ALCOHOL USE & ALCOHOLISM)

Alcohol misuse affects individuals and families alike. Recovery is possible, and support is available for both those struggling and those supporting them.

United States

- **Substance Abuse and Mental Health Services Administration (SAMHSA)**
  National Helpline: 1-800-662-HELP (4357)
  Website: SAMHSA.gov
  24/7 treatment referral and information

- **Alcoholics Anonymous (AA)**
  Website: AA.org

- **Al-Anon Family Groups**
  Website: Al-Anon.org

International

- **Findahelpline.com** for global referrals

The following books were personally meaningful during my family's healing journey:

- **Sober Curious** by Ruby Warrington

- **Quit Like a Woman** by Holly Whitaker

You did not cause the addiction. You cannot control it. You can choose support, boundaries, and care for yourself.

EATING DISORDERS
(BULIMIA / ANOREXIA / BINGE EATING)

Eating disorders are complex and serious, but recovery is possible with professional support.

United States

- **National Alliance for Eating Disorders**
  Website: AllianceForEatingDisorders.com

- **National Eating Disorders Association (NEDA)**
  Call: 1-800-931-2237
  Text: NEDA to 741741

International

- **Findahelpline.com** for global support referrals

Supporting someone does not mean fixing them. It means encouraging help, offering compassion, and knowing when professionals need to step in.

NARCISSISTIC ABUSE / RELATIONAL & VERBAL ABUSE

Emotional, verbal, and psychological abuse can leave deep wounds without visible marks.

If you experienced control, gaslighting, chronic blame-shifting, intimidation, or emotional invalidation, your experience matters.

Abuse is not defined by frequency, but by impact.

United States

- **National Domestic Violence Hotline**
  Call: 1-800-799-SAFE (7233)
  Text: START to 88788

- **Love Is Respect**
  Call: 866-331-9474
  Text: LOVEIS to 22522
  Website: LoveIsRespect.org

International

- **Findahelpline.com**

A book that helped me understand and create a plan for healing:

- **Enough is Enough** by David E. Clarke, PhD

You do not need proof, permission, or a diagnosis to seek help.

CONGENITAL HEART DEFECTS (CHDs) / HEART VALVE DISEASE

Navigating heart surgery, recovery, and long-term care can feel over-whelming. Education and community can make a profound difference.

The following resources were personally meaningful during my medical journey:

- **HeartValveSurgery.com**

- **Heart Valve Surgery:** *The Patient's Guide* by Adam Pick

Additional Support

- **Adult Congenital Heart Association (ACHA)**

- **American Heart Association (AHA)**
  Website: Heart.org

You are more than your diagnosis. Knowledge empowers. Community makes healing less lonely.

About the Author

Tammi Gunwall is a storyteller of the soul—an author, poet, and speaker who believes that everyone carries a sacred narrative worth honoring.

Her work is born not from theory or textbooks, but from the raw, lived experiences that shaped her: childhood trauma, emotional and physical abuse, spiritual questioning, heartbreak, divorce, financial instability, health battles, and the long winding road back to herself.

Through that journey, Tammi discovered the heart of her message: **healing is made of a thousand small resurrections**—moments where we rise a little, soften a little, return to ourselves a little. She learned that true joy, peace, and self-love aren't found at the finish line but in the becoming, in the courage to keep choosing wholeness one breath at a time.

She writes for the women who have felt alone in their stories, who have questioned their strength, who have forgotten their brilliance. Through her book, her *Her Soul in Ink* online messaging, and her speaking, she helps women reclaim their voice, embrace their story, and remember that they are never meant to heal alone.

Tammi is also a mother of four, grandmother of five, and woman of faith whose life reflects resilience, redemption, and the quiet courage of choosing oneself. She calls Minnesota home and finds joy in meaningful conversation, spiritual growth, and the sacred practice of honoring one's unfolding.